WILLIAMS
SONOMA
CALIFORNIA

# alfresco

125 RECIPES FOR EATING & ENJOYING OUTDOORS

weldon**owen**

# CONTENTS

# INTRODUCTION

When the weather is nice, gathering with friends and family outdoors transforms a meal into a party. From spring to fall and all the warm weather in between, eating alfresco, or "in the open air," celebrates the foods of the season. A lazy afternoon picnic in the park, a fun-filled family barbecue, a beachside bonfire, or even just dinner out on the deck—each of these settings conjures joy and happiness.

Within these pages, you'll find recipes for both classic and updated favorites—from starters and salads to mains, sides, and desserts—that are great for dining outdoors. Kick off your meal with grilled asparagus with lemon-herb mayo, summer ceviche, or delicate ricotta and pea crostini with tarragon. Vietnamese-inspired summer salad rolls or pesto chicken sandwiches would be perfect picnic fare, and a lingering lunch under a shady tree could feature herbed quinoa with green onions, cucumber, and avocado and crab cake burgers with green goddess and watercress.

Grilling takes center stage when eating outdoors. Memories of backyard barbecues featuring bone-in rib eyes with chimichurri and bacon burgers with grilled onions and roasted tomato dressing, biting into buttery-sweet Oaxacan-style corn, or saucy fingerprints left behind from mountains of smoke-kissed ribs bring up the days of summer. Round out a summer alfresco meal with slices of blackberry slab pie or big squares of s'mores brownies eaten around the firepit.

When the weather warms and in temperate climates, the opportunity to celebrate, gather, and eat the best of the season's bounty presents itself. Make the most of it with this cookbook as your guide.

# GRILLING 101

Eating outdoors often includes a grill, and whether you opt for charcoal or gas, a round kettle or a small hibachi, you'll find that few cooking tools are as versatile or handy—or can flavor food as successfully—as an outdoor grill.

### CHARCOAL GRILLS

Cooking over a live fire with charcoal is gratifying but a bit more work than a gas grill. However, the satisfaction and flavor of charcoal can't be beat. Charcoal grills come in many shapes and sizes, from small picnic grills to party-size ranch kettle models. Look for a well-built, high-grade steel grill with a lid and at least two vents to control airflow and temperature. For many, the most useful size and model is the standard 22-inch kettle. Many charcoal grills can be easily converted into smokers for slow low-heat cooking.

### LIGHTING A CHARCOAL GRILL

The easiest way to light a charcoal grill is to use a chimney starter. Lightly stuff a few sheets of wadded up newspaper in the bottom of the chimney under the rack (alternatively you can use paraffin cubes). Fill the top of the chimney starter with charcoal briquettes, then place on the lower grill rack. Light the paper or cubes and the airflow will take care of getting the coals lit. Once the coals are filled with gray ash, after about 15 minutes, carefully pour out the charcoal in the configuration you desire (see Grilling Methods, page 11). Place the cooking grate over the coals, close the lid, and let preheat for about 10 minutes. Remember to brush the cooking grate clean before using.

### GAS GRILLS

Gas grills use propane instead of charcoal to create fire and are both convenient and flexible. They can run from a no-frills cart to a gadget-filled mini kitchen. Choose a model that has at least two burners, but if you plan to do indirect cooking, three to four burners will give you better control. Models with angled metal plates covering the burners are particularly effective and reduce flare-ups. Shoot for cooking racks that are stainless steel, stainless steel with a powder paint finish, or cast iron. Some models also include smoker boxes, which are handy for low and slow barbecue, like brisket and ribs.

### LIGHTING A GAS GRILL

Turn on the gas and light the burners according to the manufacturer's instructions; it's as easy as that! Turn on each burner to high (or as many burners as needed for what you are cooking), close the lid, and let the grill preheat for 10 to 15 minutes. Remember to brush the cooking grate clean before using.

# GRILLING METHODS

Two general methods are used in grilling: direct and indirect. Direct-heat grilling is used for hot and fast grilling, or food that will be cooked directly over the fire. Indirect-heat grilling is used for foods that either cook partially over direct heat and then finish cooking off heat, or foods that are cooked entirely off heat at lower temperatures.

### DIRECT GRILLING

When food is placed directly over the fire of a charcoal grill or the heat elements of a gas grill, it cooks relatively quickly, usually in less than 20 minutes. The intense heat sears and caramelizes the surface, boosting the flavor. This is the most common type of grilling and ideal for burgers, steaks, pork chops and tenderloin, boneless chicken pieces, kebabs, fish fillets, shrimp, and vegetables. A lid will help to reduce flare-ups and control the temperature. If you plan to swab the food with a sugary sauce, do it just before it comes off the grill so the sauce doesn't burn from exposure to the intense heat.

To set up your charcoal grill for direct grilling, pour the charcoal into the center of the heat grate, or to the side, covering half to two-thirds of the grate. You can also add the charcoal to baskets and center them in the grill.

To set up your gas grill for direct grilling, turn on burners as needed for the amount of food you are grilling.

### INDIRECT GRILLING

For large cuts of meat, like whole chicken, beef or pork roasts, leg of lamb and bone-in chicken pieces, or when smoking, indirect heat is the preferred way to go. Here, the food is placed away from the heat source, so it cooks from reflected heat. Sometimes, food like a thick steak or bone-in chicken is first seared over direct heat and then moved to the indirect area to finish cooking at a lower temperature. Other cuts, like whole chicken or large roasts, cook entirely on the indirect heat area of the grill, relying only on the radiant heat to cook it.

To set up your charcoal grill for indirect grilling, arrange the hot coals on two sides of the grill so that the center of the grill bed is not delivering direct heat, or arrange the coals on one-half of the grill bed, leaving the other half free. Place the food above the indirect space and cover the grill when cooking, or according to the recipe directions.

To set up your gas grill for indirect grilling, make sure the burners underneath where the food will go are off and turn on burners on one or both sides of the indirect area. For a two-burner grill, turn on one burner and grill on the opposite side. For a three-burner grill, turn on the two outside burners, leaving the center free for indirect heat. For four- or six-burner grills, turn on the outside burners and leave the center free for indirect heat. Always grill with the lid on.

### SMOKING

Indirect-heat grilling is also used for smoking and barbecuing. When smoking foods, you cook food on low heat for a long time (usually over an hour) to break down the proteins in the meat. This is ideal for cuts like beef brisket, pork ribs, pork shoulder (for pulled pork or carnitas), and whole turkey. The grill setup is similar to the indirect grilling method, with a few additional components: smoke and steam.

To set up your charcoal grill for smoking, place a drip pan filled with water on the heat grate underneath where the food will cook; this provides the steam. Add chunks of hardwood or soaked wood chips to a foil packet pierced several times with a knife directly to the hot coals to create the smoke. Keep the temperature low and add charcoal as needed to maintain the correct temperature.

To set up your gas grill for smoking, add soaked wood chips to the smoker box. Place a small pan of water on the grate next to the food. Cook over indirect heat as directed in the recipe.

# OUTDOOR ENTERTAINING

With the arrival of pleasant weather, more people are inclined to gather outside for barbecues, picnics, and garden dining. These get-togethers are often a more relaxed and simpler way to entertain. Here are a few tips to keep your next alfresco meal both easy and beautiful.

## SERVING WITH STYLE

Even though entertaining outdoors is more casual, you'll still need plates, flatware, glasses, serving pieces, and utensils. For smaller groups, set up the table(s) in advance for starters and mains, then bring out dessert plates later on when it is closer to serving time. Or stack plates together along with flatware and napkins and invite guests to take their own place settings.

**FAMILY-STYLE DINNERS** are convivial and popular, and an easy way to serve when dining outdoors. Choose food and drinks that sit well at room temperature. Have guests pass all of the food around at once so no one has to wait long to fill their plate. Wrap dishes in a dish towel or set on a trivet in the middle of the table where everyone can reach.

**BUFFETS** are an easy way to serve outside, because food can be arranged on a picnic table or folding table and guests can serve themselves. Stack plates at the beginning of the buffet line and flatware and napkins at the end so people have a free hand to load their plates; consider wrapping flatware in napkins so it is easier to pick up and carry.

**DRINKS, APPETIZERS, AND DESSERTS** can all be easily served from a separate table, keeping larger tables free for the main event. Roll out a bar cart from inside or use a potting bench for extra serving space. For drinks, include glassware and ice for ease of serving. Keep extra ice on hand in a separate cooler.

**FOR PICNICS AND BARBECUES,** you may be eating in an area outside with no table. Choose a menu that can be served on one plate and provide napkins that are big enough to spread on laps. Handheld food or food that doesn't require being cut with a knife while balancing a plate on your knees are great choices. Provide seating and make lounging comfortable with throw pillows, blankets, or even upside-down produce carts.

## CREATING A BEAUTIFUL ENVIRONMENT

Eating outside can be as uncomplicated or as glamorous as you would like. Here are some effortless ideas for creating a beautiful space for you and your guests, regardless of whether you are hosting an intimate evening fête or or an afternoon barbecue.

**DECORATE THE TABLE(S)** with flowers or greenery from the garden or add bowls of seasonal fruit or vegetables, flowering tree branches in pitchers, herb bouquets in bell jars, or small succulent plants in miniature pots.

**ADD A SPLASH OF COLOR** by using multicolored linen napkins tied with string. Colorful plates and cups or tablecloths are also festive and great for outdoor gatherings. Table runners are a good way to add color and make a table feel more intimate.

**ADD SUBTLE LIGHTING** to an evening gathering by placing clusters of candles or tea lights on the dining table. If it's windy, place candles in hurricanes to keep them lit. Strings of patio lights and paper lanterns are also great ways to light up an evening.

**USE JELLY JARS AS GLASSES** and you can even transport drinks in them with the tops screwed on for picnic-ready sipping.

**SERVE ON A VARIETY OF VESSELS,** like large cutting boards, platters, wide shallow bowls, and more.

**PUT TOGETHER A PLAYLIST** of fun, upbeat music to keep the party going. Play it on a wireless portable speaker so you can move it around at ease.

**KEEP BUGS AND INSECTS AWAY** with natural citronella candles. Bunches of fresh mint and rosemary or pots of marigolds also will help to keep those critters at bay.

starters

# Tomato Gazpacho with Bell Peppers, Cucumber & Avocado

Chilled tomato soup—embellished with roasted peppers, cucumbers, and a splash of vinegar—is a perfect way to beat the heat of summer and use up any overripe tomatoes in the summer months when they are bountiful. This Spanish classic can be served in shot glasses as an elegant appetizer or as a light lunch with crusty bread on the side. Garnish the soup with diced avocado, cucumber, and crunchy croutons with a drizzle of olive oil.

2 red bell peppers

5 lb (2.3 kg) tomatoes, preferably heirloom

8-inch (20-cm) piece English cucumber, peeled, seeded, and coarsely chopped

2 cloves garlic, coarsely chopped

¼ cup (2 fl oz/60 ml) extra-virgin olive oil, plus more for finishing

2 teaspoons sherry vinegar

Kosher salt and freshly ground pepper

1 large avocado, pitted, peeled, and chopped

**MAKES 8 SERVINGS**

Using tongs, hold 1 bell pepper over the flame of a gas burner, turning it as needed, until charred and blistered on all sides. Repeat with the second pepper. Alternatively, preheat the broiler, place the peppers on a baking sheet, and broil, turning as needed, until blackened on all sides. Place the bell peppers in a small bowl, cover the bowl with plastic wrap, and leave until cool. Peel off the blackened skin and remove the stem and seeds. Set aside.

Bring a large saucepan three-fourths full of water to a boil over medium-high heat. Using a small, sharp knife, cut out the stem from each tomato, then cut a small, shallow X on the blossom end. Working in small batches, immerse the tomatoes in the boiling water until the skins blister, about 30 seconds. As they are ready, using a slotted spoon, transfer the tomatoes to a large colander.

Working over a bowl, peel the tomatoes, discarding the skins. Using your fingers, break the tomatoes open and gently squeeze and scrape the seeds and juices into the bowl. Place the flesh in another bowl. Using a fine-mesh sieve, strain the juices into the bowl with the tomato flesh. Discard the seeds.

Working in batches, in a blender, combine the tomato flesh and juice, roasted bell peppers, cucumber, garlic, olive oil, vinegar, and salt and pepper to taste. Process until smooth, then transfer to an airtight container. Refrigerate until well chilled, about 2 hours.

Taste and adjust the seasoning, if needed, then divide among chilled bowls. Garnish with the avocado, drizzle with a little olive oil, and serve.

# Chilled Cucumber-Yogurt Soup with Lemon & Mint

This Mediterranean soup is delicious and refreshing with its base of delicately flavored cucumber and yogurt. Fresh mint, lemon juice, and garlic add layers of flavor. It's excellent on its own, or served alongside a meal of grilled cumin-spiced lamb chops or lamb burgers and fluffy herbed couscous.

6 large English cucumbers, about 5 lb (2.3 kg) total, peeled and seeded

8 tablespoons (1 oz/30 g) minced fresh mint

4 tablespoons (2 fl oz/60 ml) extra-virgin olive oil

Finely grated zest and juice of 1 large lemon

4 cups (32 fl oz/1 l) chicken broth

4 cups (2 lb/1 kg) plain yogurt

2 small cloves garlic, minced

Kosher salt and freshly ground pepper

**MAKES 8 TO 10 SERVINGS**

Finely chop 1 cucumber. Place half of the pieces between layers of paper towels, pressing to absorb excess moisture. Transfer to a small bowl, add 2 tablespoons of the mint and 1 tablespoon of the olive oil, and toss to combine. Cover and refrigerate until ready to use. Cut the remaining 5 cucumbers into large chunks.

Working in batches, in a food processor or blender, coarsely purée the cucumber chunks, the remaining 6 tablespoons of mint, the lemon zest, and 2 cups (16 fl oz/ 475 ml) of the broth. Transfer the mixture to a large nonreactive bowl. Add the remaining 2 cups (16 fl oz/475 ml) of broth, the reserved cucumber-mint mixture, the remaining 3 tablespoons of olive oil, the lemon juice, yogurt, and garlic. Add 1½ teaspoons of salt and season with pepper. Stir to blend well, cover, and refrigerate until well chilled, at least 4 hours or up to 12 hours. Serve.

# Smoky Roasted Eggplant Dip with Cumin-Crusted Pita

This easy Middle Eastern dip, also known as baba ghanoush, is a snap to make. Roasted eggplant and garlic give the dish it's telltale smoky flavor, and tahini adds creamy richness. A splash of lemon juice and a sprinkle of smoked paprika highlight the delicate flavors of the dip. Serve with crunchy homemade pita bread, or purchase pita chips for an even easier presentation.

**PITA CHIPS**

1 teaspoon cumin seeds

Kosher salt

3 pita breads, 7 inches (18 cm) in diameter

1½ tablespoons extra-virgin olive oil

**EGGPLANT DIP**

6 cloves garlic, unpeeled, ends trimmed

1 teaspoon extra-virgin olive oil, plus more for brushing

2 Italian eggplants, about 2 lb (1 kg) total, halved lengthwise

2 tablespoons fresh lemon juice

¼ cup (2¼ oz/60 g) tahini

Kosher salt

½ teaspoon smoked paprika

**MAKES 6 SERVINGS**

Preheat the oven to 400°F (200°C). Line a baking sheet with aluminum foil.

To make the pita chips, in a small frying pan over medium heat, toast the cumin seeds, stirring frequently, until fragrant, about 2 minutes. Pour onto a plate to cool. Transfer the cumin seeds to a spice mill or mortar, add ¾ teaspoon of salt, and grind or crush with a pestle until finely ground.

Brush the pita breads on both sides with oil, then cut each pita into 8 wedges. Arrange the wedges on the prepared baking sheet. Sprinkle the tops evenly with the cumin mixture. Bake until the wedges are light golden brown and crisp, 10–15 minutes, turning them over halfway through baking. Set aside.

To make the eggplant dip, place the garlic cloves on a small square of aluminum foil, drizzle with the 1 teaspoon of olive oil, and wrap securely in the foil. Place on the baking sheet and bake until the garlic is soft, about 15 minutes. Unwrap and let stand until cool enough to handle.

Preheat the broiler. Line the baking sheet with aluminum foil and lightly grease with olive oil. Place the eggplants on the prepared baking sheet, cut side down, and broil until the skins char and the flesh is tender, about 20 minutes. Transfer the eggplants to a colander and set it in the sink to drain and cool slightly.

Using a spoon, scrape the eggplant flesh out of the skins into a blender. Squeeze the roasted garlic from its skins and add to the blender along with the lemon juice, tahini, and a pinch of salt. Blend the ingredients until smooth, then taste and season with additional salt, if needed. Transfer the dip to a serving bowl and let stand for a few minutes to allow the flavors to blend. Sprinkle the dip with the paprika and place on a platter. Arrange the pita chips alongside and serve.

# Grilled Oysters with Herb Butter & Barbecue Sauce

Freshly shucked oysters taste like the ocean. They are amazing raw, but their subtle briny flavor is enhanced by a short visit to the grill, bathed in herb-scented butter and a drizzle of barbecue sauce. Choose medium or medium-large oysters—if they are too small they are difficult to grill, and if they are too large they are difficult to slurp.

**HERB BUTTER**

¼ cup (2 oz/60 g) unsalted butter, at cool room temperature

2 teaspoons *each* minced fresh flat-leaf parsley, chervil, tarragon, and chives

¼ teaspoon kosher salt and freshly ground pepper

24 medium or medium-large oysters

¼ cup (2 fl oz/60 ml) Classic Barbecue Sauce (page 175), or your favorite barbecue sauce

6 lemon wedges

**MAKES 6 SERVINGS**

To make the herb butter, in a bowl, using a fork, stir together the butter, parsley, chervil, tarragon, chives, ¼ teaspoon of salt, and pepper to taste, mixing well. Transfer the mixture to a sheet of plastic wrap and, using a rubber spatula and the plastic wrap, shape the butter into a log about 1½ inches (4 cm) in diameter. Wrap the log in the plastic wrap and refrigerate until firm, about 30 minutes, or store in the refrigerator for up to 1 week.

To shuck the oysters, working with 1 oyster at a time and holding it with the flat side up, press a sturdy, dull knife between the hinged end of the shell to pop the top and bottom shells apart. Run the knife along the inside of the top (flatter) shell to cut the meat from the shell and then lift off the top shell, holding the bottom oyster shell level to retain its liquor (juices). Run the knife under the oyster to detach it from the bottom (rounded) shell, but leave the oyster nestled in the liquor in the shell. Pick out any bits of shell. The liquor should be clear. If it's cloudy, the oyster is older and has begun to break down, and it should be discarded.

Prepare a gas or charcoal grill for direct grilling over medium heat (350°–450°F/ 180°–230°C). Brush the grill grate clean. Place the oysters directly on the grate and top each oyster with about ½ teaspoon of the herb butter and ½ teaspoon of barbecue sauce. Grill until the oyster shells char on the edges, 8–10 minutes.

Transfer the oysters to a platter. Serve hot with the lemon wedges for squeezing.

# Summer Ceviche with Avocado

Ceviche, a refreshingly tangy South American fish dish, is made from curing raw fish in citrus juices. It's important to use the freshest fish possible, so try to purchase it from a trusted fish market and make sure it smells pleasantly briny. Diced mango would be a terrific addition to this ceviche for a hint of sweetness.

1 lb (450 g) boneless firm white fish, such as snapper or halibut, cut into ½-inch (12-mm) pieces

1 cup (8 fl oz/240 ml) fresh lime juice

¼ cup (1½ oz/40 g) minced white onion

1 red jalapeño chile, minced

1 avocado, pitted, peeled, and diced

¼ cup (½ oz/15 g) minced fresh cilantro

2 tablespoons minced fresh mint

Kosher salt and freshly ground pepper

Tortilla chips, for serving

**MAKES 6 SERVINGS**

In a nonreactive bowl, stir together the fish, lime juice, onion, and jalapeño. Cover and refrigerate until the fish is opaque throughout, 30–60 minutes.

Using a slotted spoon, transfer the fish, onion, and jalapeño to another bowl, reserving the marinade. To the fish, add the avocado, cilantro, mint, and a pinch each of salt and pepper. Add some of the marinade for more acidity, if needed. Stir gently to mix and serve right away with tortilla chips.

# Grilled Vegetable Antipasti

An array of grilled summer vegetables, drizzled with olive oil, vinegar, garlic, and parsley, is a deliciously simple and versatile addition to any summer feast. It can serve as a starter, a vegetarian main dish, or a side dish to grilled fish, chicken, or steak. For an elegant presentation, arrange the grilled vegetables on a serving platter alongside creamy burrata or fresh mozzarella cheese and grilled country-style bread.

2 cloves garlic

½ cup (½ oz/15 g) fresh flat-leaf parsley leaves

½ cup (4 fl oz/120 ml) extra-virgin olive oil, plus 2 tablespoons for brushing

2 teaspoons red wine vinegar

1 Italian eggplant, about 1 lb (450 g), trimmed and cut crosswise into slices ½ inch (12 mm) thick

2 zucchini, trimmed and thickly sliced lengthwise

2 red or yellow bell peppers

6 green onions, including tender green tops, trimmed

Kosher salt

½ teaspoon red pepper flakes (optional)

**MAKES 6 SERVINGS**

Prepare a gas or charcoal grill for direct grilling over medium-high heat (400°–450°F/200°–230°C). Brush the grill grate clean.

Using a chef's knife, mince together the garlic and parsley. Transfer to a small bowl, add the ½ cup (4 fl oz/120 ml) of olive oil and the vinegar, and mix well. Set aside.

Brush the vegetables with the remaining 2 tablespoons of olive oil. Grill the eggplant, zucchini slices, peppers, and green onions over direct heat, turning once with tongs, until both sides have grill marks and the slices are tender, about 6 minutes total for the eggplant and about 3 minutes total for the zucchini. Grill the green onions, turning as needed, until slightly charred and tender, about 4 minutes total. Grill the peppers, turning as needed, until the skin is blackened and evenly blistered on all sides, about 10 minutes total.

As the vegetables finish cooking, transfer them to a platter. Place the peppers in a paper bag and fold the top over so they will steam. Set aside until cool enough to handle, then remove from the bag, remove and discard the stems, and slit the peppers open lengthwise and remove and discard the seeds and ribs. Peel away the blackened skin, and cut the peppers lengthwise into strips about ½ inch (12 mm) wide. Add the pepper strips to the platter.

Drizzle the olive oil–parsley mixture evenly over the vegetables, and then sprinkle with salt and red pepper flakes, if using. Serve at once.

# Grilled Asparagus with Lemon-Herb Mayonnaise

The grill adds a smoky char to tender asparagus spears, making grilling an ideal cooking method for the spring vegetable. Choose thicker spears and line them up perpendicular to the grill grate so they don't fall through the cracks. The homemade mayo is not only delicious with asparagus but also excellent when used on sandwiches or as a dip for sweet potato fries.

**LEMON-HERB MAYONNAISE**

1 large egg yolk

1 tablespoon Dijon mustard

1 clove garlic, minced

3 tablespoons avocado or canola oil

3 tablespoons extra-virgin olive oil

2 teaspoons fresh lemon juice

1 teaspoon finely grated lemon zest

Kosher salt and freshly ground pepper

1 tablespoon minced fresh chives

1 tablespoon minced fresh flat-leaf parsley

1½ lb (680 g) asparagus spears, trimmed

1½ tablespoons extra-virgin olive oil

1 teaspoon finely grated lemon zest

Kosher salt and freshly ground pepper

2 tablespoons snipped fresh chives

2 tablespoons fresh flat-leaf parsley leaves

**MAKES 6 SERVINGS**

To make the mayonnaise, in a small, deep bowl, vigorously whisk together the egg yolk, mustard, and garlic until blended. Combine the avocado and olive oils in a small measuring pitcher. Drizzle about 2 teaspoons of the oil mixture over the egg mixture and whisk vigorously for about 30 seconds to blend thoroughly. Repeat two more times, at which point the mixture should be emulsified. In a slow, steady stream, add the remaining oil mixture while whisking constantly. Continue to whisk until the mayonnaise thickens to a spreadable consistency. Whisk in the lemon juice and zest and season with salt and pepper. Stir in the chives and parsley. Set aside while you grill the asparagus, or cover and refrigerate for up to 4 days.

Prepare a gas or charcoal grill for direct grilling over medium heat (350°–450°F/ 180°–230°C). Brush the grill grate clean. Spread the asparagus on a rimmed baking sheet. Drizzle with the olive oil, sprinkle with the lemon zest, and season with salt and pepper, then toss to coat. Arrange the asparagus on the grill directly over the heat and grill, turning occasionally, until crisp-tender, about 2 minutes.

Transfer the asparagus to a platter. Garnish with the chives and parsley and serve, passing the mayonnaise at the table.

# Deviled Eggs with Lemon Zest & Parsley

This simple twist on classic deviled eggs is perfect for a small gathering, or double the recipe for a picnic or potluck. The addition of lemon zest and fresh parsley adds zing and an earthy note. For a more traditional version, omit the zest and herbs, substitute yellow mustard for the Dijon, and add 2 teaspoons of minced pickle relish.

6 large eggs, at room temperature

2 tablespoons mayonnaise

1 teaspoon Dijon mustard

1 tablespoon chopped fresh flat-leaf parsley, plus more for garnish

½ teaspoon finely grated lemon zest

Kosher salt and freshly ground pepper

**MAKES 6 SERVINGS**

Prepare a large bowl of ice water. Gently place the eggs in a saucepan and add tepid water to cover by about 2 inches (5 cm). Bring to a boil over high heat, then reduce the heat to low and simmer, uncovered, for 10 minutes. Using a slotted spoon, transfer the eggs to the ice bath and set aside until cool.

Carefully peel the eggs and halve lengthwise. Remove the yolks and put them in a small bowl. Place the whites, cavity side up, on a serving plate.

Add the mayonnaise and mustard to the bowl with the yolks. Using a fork, mash and mix the yolks to form a paste. Stir in the parsley and lemon zest. Season with salt and pepper. Spoon the yolk mixture into the cavities of the egg whites, dividing it evenly and mounding it in the center. Alternatively, spoon the yolk mixture into a pastry bag fitted with a large plain or star tip and pipe the mixture into the whites. Garnish with parsley and pepper and serve right away.

# Roasted Tomato Salsa & Guacamole with Chips

Homemade roasted tomato salsa and creamy guacamole are quick to make and surpass anything you can purchase at a grocery store. The salsa makes use of summer's fresh tomatoes, but when they are out of season, substitute a 14-ounce (400-g) can of fire-roasted diced tomatoes. Choose ripe avocados that have a little give so they are creamy when mashed.

**ROASTED TOMATO SALSA**

1 lb (450 g) ripe plum tomatoes

1 jalapeño chile

3 cloves garlic, unpeeled

½ white onion, quartered

2 teaspoons extra-virgin olive oil

⅓ cup (⅓ oz/10 g) loosely packed fresh cilantro, chopped

1 teaspoon red wine vinegar

Kosher salt

**GUACAMOLE**

3 ripe avocados, pitted and peeled

3 tablespoons chopped fresh cilantro

Juice of 1 lime

Hot sauce, such as Tabasco (optional)

Kosher salt and freshly ground pepper

Tortilla chips, for serving

**MAKES 6 TO 8 SERVINGS**

To make the salsa, position a rack about 6 inches (15 cm) from the broiler and preheat the broiler. Line a rimmed baking sheet with aluminum foil. Cut the tomatoes in half lengthwise and place the halves, cut side down, on the prepared baking sheet. Place the jalapeño, garlic, and onion on the baking sheet, arranging them in a single, uncrowded layer. Drizzle with the olive oil. Broil, turning the vegetables once and rotating the baking sheet as needed, until the vegetables are charred all over, about 5 minutes per side. Remove from the oven and let cool.

When cool enough to handle, seed the jalapeño and peel the garlic. Combine the tomatoes, jalapeño, garlic, onion, and cilantro in a blender or food processor. Process until well combined and there are no large chunks, but the salsa still has plenty of texture. Add the vinegar and pulse to combine. Season with salt. The salsa can be stored in an airtight container in the refrigerator for up to 1 week.

To make the guacamole, scoop the flesh from the avocados into a bowl. Using a potato masher or a large fork, smash the avocados until mostly smooth. Stir in the cilantro, lime juice, and a few dashes of hot sauce, if using. Season with salt and pepper. To store, press plastic wrap directly onto the surface of the guacamole and tightly around the bowl, and refrigerate for up to 1 day.

Serve the salsa and guacamole with chips alongside for dipping.

# Chicken Satay with Spicy Peanut Sauce

A popular Southeast Asian street food, satay consists of tender skewers of grilled marinated meat served with a sauce such as sweet soy sauce or peanut sauce. Chicken satay with peanut sauce is a popular version, and this recipe is particularly delicious. The homemade peanut sauce is well worth making, but in a pinch you can use a purchased version.

**CHICKEN SATAY**

1 cup (8 fl oz/240 ml) coconut milk

¼ cup (2 fl oz/60 ml) fish sauce

4 cloves garlic, minced

¼ cup (½ oz/15 g) minced fresh cilantro

1 teaspoon curry powder

Freshly ground pepper

4 lb (1.8 kg) boneless, skinless chicken breasts

16 to 20 wooden skewers, soaked in water for 30 minutes

**SPICY PEANUT SAUCE**

2 cups (16 fl oz/475 ml) coconut milk

¼ cup (1½ oz/40 g) chopped unsalted dry-roasted peanuts

2 tablespoons all-natural creamy peanut butter

2 tablespoons firmly packed light brown sugar

2 tablespoons fish sauce

1 tablespoon tamarind paste or 1 teaspoon fresh lime juice

1½ teaspoons green curry paste

1 teaspoon sweet paprika

1 clove garlic, minced, then crushed to a paste

**MAKES 6 TO 8 SERVINGS**

To make the to make the marinade for the chicken satay, in a bowl, stir together the coconut milk, fish sauce, garlic, cilantro, curry powder, and 1 teaspoon of pepper. Set aside.

One at a time, place the chicken breasts between 2 sheets of plastic wrap, and lightly pound with a meat pounder or rolling pin to an even thickness of about ½ inch (12 mm). Then, using a sharp knife, cut each breast lengthwise into 3 or 4 strips. Add the chicken strips to the marinade and refrigerate for at least 4 hours or up to 8 hours.

To make the spicy peanut sauce, in a saucepan over medium heat, combine the coconut milk, peanuts, peanut butter, brown sugar, fish sauce, tamarind paste, curry paste, paprika, and garlic. Bring to a gentle simmer, stirring constantly to blend the ingredients thoroughly, then cook, stirring occasionally, until thickened and reduced by half, 15–20 minutes. Remove from the heat and set aside.

At least 30 minutes before you are ready to begin grilling, remove the chicken from the refrigerator. Discard the marinade and pat the chicken strips dry with paper towels.

Prepare a gas or charcoal grill for direct grilling over high heat (450°–550°F/230°–290°C). Brush the grill grate clean.

Thread the chicken strips lengthwise onto the skewers. Place on the grill and cook, turning once, until the chicken is grill-marked on both sides and opaque throughout but still moist, about 4 minutes on each side.

Arrange the skewers on a platter and let rest for about 5 minutes before serving. Pass the peanut sauce at the table.

# Honey-Sesame Glazed Chicken Wings

These sweet and spicy wings are irresistible and will be popular at any gathering. The glaze—made of sweet-hot chile sauce, sesame oil, honey, teriyaki, and shichimi togarashi—unites some of the greatest Japanese flavors into one amazing starter. Shichimi togarashi is a blend of chile, sesame seeds, seaweed, citrus rind, and other ingredients and can be found at most well-stocked markets.

3 lb (1.4 kg) chicken wings, tips removed

¼ cup (2 fl oz/60 ml) canola oil

2 tablespoons shichimi togarashi spice blend

¾ cup (6 fl oz/180 ml) sweet-hot chile sauce

¼ cup (2 fl oz/60 ml) teriyaki sauce

2 tablespoons honey

2 tablespoons toasted sesame oil

Juice of 1 lime

2 tablespoons sesame seeds, toasted (optional)

**MAKES 6 TO 8 SERVINGS**

In a large bowl, combine the chicken wings and oil and toss until the wings are evenly coated. Sprinkle the shichimi togarashi spice blend over the wings and toss again to coat evenly. Set aside at room temperature for about 30 minutes.

Prepare a gas or charcoal grill for direct grilling over medium-high heat (400°–450°F/200°–230°C). Brush the grill grate clean.

To make the glaze, in a small saucepan, stir together the chile sauce, teriyaki sauce, honey, and sesame oil. Place over low heat and bring to a gentle simmer, stirring. Remove from the heat and let cool slightly. Stir in the lime juice. Set aside at room temperature.

Place the chicken wings on the grill and cook, turning frequently, until they are nicely browned on all sides, have some char, and are cooked through and tender, 15–20 minutes.

Transfer the wings to a large bowl, pour the glaze over them, and toss to coat evenly. Let sit for about 5 minutes to allow the flavors to meld, then transfer to a platter, sprinkle with the sesame seeds, if using, and serve at once.

# Grilled Figs with Prosciutto

Fresh figs have a fleeting season in the early and late summer months, but when they are available, grilling them is an excellent way to showcase their delicate sweetness. Black Mission figs are a great choice because of their rich, deep flavor, but other types of figs work well, too. Be sure to select ripe figs that give a little when gently pressed and use them right away.

4 ripe figs, such as
Black Mission

4–6 thin slices prosciutto

¼ cup (1¼ oz/30 g) fresh goat cheese, at room temperature

Extra-virgin olive oil,
for brushing

Kosher salt and freshly
ground pepper

2 tablespoons balsamic
vinegar or balsamic syrup

2 tablespoons honey

**MAKES 6 TO 8 SERVINGS**

Cut the figs in half lengthwise, or into quarters, depending on their size. Lay the prosciutto slices flat on a work surface. With a sharp knife, cut each slice crosswise into 4 pieces. Spoon about 1 teaspoon of goat cheese on top of each fig half, then tightly wrap the piece of prosciutto around the fig. Secure the bundles with toothpicks, if necessary.

Prepare a gas or charcoal grill for direct and indirect grilling over medium-high heat (400°–450°F/200°–230°C). Brush the grill grate clean.

Lightly brush the fig bundles with olive oil and season with salt and pepper. Grill the bundles directly over the heat, turning often, until grill-marked on all sides, 4–6 minutes total. Move the bundles to indirect heat and drizzle with the balsamic vinegar. Grill, covered, until the figs are cooked through and the cheese melts, about 3 minutes longer.

Transfer the fig bundles to a serving plate, drizzle with the honey, and serve hot.

# Ricotta & Pea Crostini with Tarragon

The whipped pea, green garlic, tarragon, and ricotta topping for these crunchy crostini evokes the flavors of spring. Early spring peas are sweet and delicate, so be sure to choose the smallest peas you can find before they become overly starchy. Choose a regular or whole-grain baguette, and for the prettiest presentation, garnish with the fresh tarragon leaves and pink peppercorns.

2 tablespoons extra-virgin olive oil, plus more for brushing

1 green onion, thinly sliced

1 tablespoon finely sliced green garlic or 1 clove garlic, minced

1½ cups (6½ oz/185 g) fresh English peas, shelled

1½ tablespoons minced fresh tarragon leaves, plus whole leaves for garnish

Kosher salt and freshly ground pepper

¾ cup (6 oz/170 g) ricotta cheese

½ cup (2 oz/60 g) freshly grated Parmesan cheese

24 thin slices baguette

1 tablespoon pink peppercorns, for garnish (optional)

**MAKES 24 CROSTINI**

Preheat the oven to 400°F (200°C). In a heavy frying pan over medium heat, warm the 2 tablespoons of olive oil. Add the green onion and green garlic and cook until tender, about 1 minute. Add the peas and tarragon and stir to coat. Add 6 tablespoons (3 fl oz/90 ml) of water and a sprinkle of salt and cook until the peas are tender and almost all of the water has evaporated, about 7 minutes. Remove from the heat and let cool slightly.

Transfer to a food processor, add the ricotta and Parmesan, and process until smooth. Season with salt and pepper. (The mixture can be covered and refrigerated for up to 2 days.)

Arrange the baguette slices on a large baking sheet. Brush the slices lightly with olive oil. Place in the oven until lightly toasted, about 8 minutes.

Spread the toasts thickly with the purée and return to the baking sheet. Return to the oven and heat just until the purée is warmed through, about 7 minutes.

Arrange the crostini on a platter, sprinkle with tarragon leaves and peppercorns, if using, and serve.

# Caponata Bruschetta

Caponata—a sweet and sour mixture of olive oil–fried eggplant, bell peppers, olives, and capers—is an iconic Sicilian antipasti and makes an excellent starter when served atop grilled bread. The flavors improve when allowed to sit overnight so it's an ideal dish to make in advance. Serve at room temperature.

**CAPONATA**

Extra-virgin olive oil, for frying

2 lb (1 kg) small Italian eggplants, trimmed and cut into 1-inch (2.5-cm) cubes

2 red or yellow bell peppers, seeded and cut into ½-inch (12-mm) squares

2 yellow onions, diced

3 small inner ribs celery, sliced

3 ripe tomatoes, seeded and chopped

1 cup (5 oz/140 g) chopped pitted green olives

⅓ cup (2 oz/60 g) raisins or currants

2 tablespoons capers, rinsed and drained

2 tablespoons sugar

2 tablespoons red wine vinegar

Kosher salt

¼ cup (¾ oz/25 g) sliced almonds, toasted

**BRUSCHETTA**

8 slices coarse country bread, about ½ inch (12 mm) thick

2 cloves garlic, peeled and left whole

¼ cup (2 fl oz/60 ml) extra-virgin olive oil

**MAKES 8 SERVINGS**

To make the caponata, pour the olive oil to a depth of ½ inch (12 mm) into a deep, heavy frying pan and place over medium heat until hot. The oil is ready when an eggplant cube dropped into it sizzles on impact. Line a large platter or tray with paper towels and set it next to the stove.

Working in batches, arrange the eggplant cubes in the pan in a single layer, being careful not to crowd them. Cook, stirring occasionally, until the eggplant is tender and browned, 7–8 minutes. Using a slotted spoon, transfer to the prepared platter to drain. Repeat with the remaining eggplant.

When all of the eggplant has been cooked, fry the bell peppers in the same way until tender and lightly browned, 4–6 minutes, and drain on paper towels as well. Finally, fry the onions and celery together in the same way until tender and golden, 7–8 minutes, and drain on paper towels.

In a large saucepan over low heat, combine the tomatoes, olives, raisins, capers, sugar, and vinegar. Stir well and add the fried vegetables and a pinch of salt. Cover partially and cook, stirring occasionally, until the mixture thickens, about 20 minutes. Add a little water if the mixture begins to dry out. Remove from the heat, transfer to a serving dish, and let cool to room temperature. Season with more salt if needed. If time permits, cover and refrigerate overnight to allow the flavors to marry; bring to room temperature before serving.

Just before serving, sprinkle the almonds over the top.

To make the bruschetta, prepare a gas or charcoal grill for direct grilling over medium-high heat (400°–450°F/200°–230°C). Brush the grill grate clean. Alternatively, preheat a grill pan over medium-high heat on the stovetop. Grill the bread, turning once with tongs, until crisp and golden on both sides, about 3 minutes total. Remove from the heat and immediately rub one side of each slice vigorously with a garlic clove, using 1 clove for 4 slices. Arrange the bread slices, garlic side up, on a serving platter. Spoon the caponata on the bread, dividing it evenly. Drizzle with the olive oil. Serve at once.

# Grilled Shishito Peppers with Sea Salt

Small, green shishitos are a mildly spicy, flavorful pepper that are terrific when blistered on a grill or in a hot cast-iron pan. But beware—occasionally a hot one sneaks into a batch. They need nothing more than a sprinkling of salt to bring out their earthiness, but a pinch of bonito flakes would also be a welcome accompaniment.

1 lb (450 g) shishito peppers

1 lemon, halved

1 tablespoon extra-virgin olive oil

Flaky sea salt

**MAKES 6 TO 8 SERVINGS**

Prepare a gas or charcoal grill for direct grilling over high heat (450°–550°F/230°–290°C). Brush the grill grate clean.

In a bowl, toss the peppers and lemon halves with the olive oil. Grill the peppers and lemons, turning as needed, until charred on all sides, 3–4 minutes total. Season with salt and serve, squeezing the lemon juice over the peppers.

# salads

# Spicy Thai Steak Salad with Herbs

Thinly sliced flank steak is best when cooked to medium—too rare and it's chewy, too well-done and it becomes dry. Here it is served atop a bed of fresh lettuce with plenty of crunchy vegetables, verdant herbs, and a well-balanced, sweet-spicy-salty dressing. You can adjust the heat level by adding more (or fewer) chiles to the dressing.

**VINAIGRETTE**

3 tablespoons Thai fish sauce

3 tablespoons fresh lime juice

2 teaspoons sugar

1–2 teaspoons minced fresh Thai chiles

1 lb (450 g) flank steak

Kosher salt and freshly ground pepper

2 teaspoons canola oil

1 large head butter lettuce or red leaf lettuce, leaves torn into bite-size pieces

1 cup (5 oz/140 g) thinly sliced English cucumber

½ cup (1¾ oz/50 g) thinly sliced red onion

½ cup (2½ oz/70 g) red bell pepper strips

½ cup (1 oz/30 g) chopped fresh mint

½ cup (1 oz/30 g) chopped fresh cilantro

¼ cup (½ oz/15 g) chopped fresh basil, preferably Thai

**MAKES 4 SERVINGS**

To make the vinaigrette, in a large bowl, whisk together the fish sauce, lime juice, sugar, and chiles. Set aside.

Prepare a gas or charcoal grill for direct grilling over high heat (450°–550°F/230°–290°C). Brush the grill grate clean.

Season the flank steak all over with salt and pepper. Brush both sides with the oil. Place the flank steak directly over the heat and grill, turning once, until seared on the outside and cooked rare to medium-rare in the center, about 4 minutes per side. (Alternatively, place the flank steak on a broiler pan and broil, turning once, until the meat is seared on the outside and cooked rare to medium-rare in the center, about 4 minutes per side.)

Transfer the steak to a cutting board, tent with aluminum foil, and let rest for 20 minutes.

Cut the steak across the grain on the diagonal into very thin slices. Add the slices to the vinaigrette and toss to coat. Add the lettuce, cucumber, onion, bell pepper, mint, cilantro, and basil and toss to coat. Serve right away.

# Chopped Salad with Tarragon-Buttermilk Dressing

A successful chopped salad consists of a variety of vegetables, greens, and sometimes, meats and cheeses, chopped into small uniform pieces before being tossed with a tangy-creamy dressing. Endlessly versatile, this technique is a great way to use up salad ingredients or other leftovers. Try adding marinated artichoke hearts, salami or rotisserie chicken, and mozzarella cheese for an even heartier meal.

**TARRAGON-BUTTERMILK DRESSING**

2 tablespoons minced garlic

2 tablespoons minced shallot

5 tablespoons (3 oz/90 g) sour cream

¼ cup (2 fl oz/60 ml) buttermilk

2 tablespoons fresh lemon juice

2 teaspoons chopped fresh tarragon

Kosher salt and freshly ground pepper

1 heart romaine lettuce, cored and chopped

1 small head radicchio, cored and chopped

1 small cucumber, peeled and chopped

8 radishes, chopped

1½ cups (9 oz/250 g) cherry tomatoes, quartered

1 cup (5 oz/140 g) hazelnuts, toasted and chopped

**MAKES 6 SERVINGS**

To make the dressing, in a bowl, combine the garlic, shallot, sour cream, buttermilk, lemon juice, tarragon, ½ teaspoon of salt, and ¼ teaspoon of pepper and whisk to blend well. Set aside.

In a large salad bowl, combine the romaine, radicchio, cucumber, radishes, tomatoes, and hazelnuts and toss to mix. Drizzle the dressing over the salad and toss to coat all the ingredients well. Taste and adjust the seasoning, if needed. Serve right away.

# Summer Salad Rolls with Nuoc Cham

These fresh rolls are stuffed with rice noodles, a variety of salad ingredients, and strips of tofu then wrapped in soft rice-paper rounds. They are excellent on a hot day when you don't want to use the oven or stovetop. Instead of tofu you can add poached shrimp or leftover marinated grilled pork. Nuoc cham is a sweet-spicy-tangy sauce and a staple of Vietnamese cuisine, but you can also serve these with spicy peanut sauce (page 30).

**NUOC CHAM**

3 cloves garlic, minced

1½ tablespoons sugar

3 tablespoons fish sauce

2 tablespoons rice vinegar

2 tablespoons fresh lime juice

½ serrano chile, seeded and very thinly sliced

2 tablespoons grated carrot

8 rice-paper rounds, each 12 inches (30 cm) in diameter

2 oz (60 g) cellophane noodles

8 red leaf lettuce leaves, stems removed

1 carrot, peeled and finely shredded

½ small cucumber, peeled, seeded, and finely shredded

½-lb (8 oz/225 g) block extra-firm tofu, cut into 16 slices, each 4 inches (10 cm) long by ¼ inch (6 mm) thick

½ cup (2 oz/60 g) mung bean sprouts

Leaves from 1 bunch fresh mint

Leaves from 1 bunch fresh cilantro

**MAKES 4 TO 6 SERVINGS**

To make the nuoc cham, using a mortar and pestle, grind together the garlic and sugar until a paste forms (or combine the ingredients in a mini food processor and process to a paste). Transfer to a bowl and whisk in the fish sauce, vinegar, lime juice, and ¼ cup (2 fl oz/60 ml) water. Pour through a fine-mesh sieve into a bowl, then add the chile and carrot. You should have about ⅔ cup.

Working with 1 rice-paper round at a time, soak the round in warm water. Soak the noodles in warm water for 15 minutes or according to package directions; drain.

To assemble each roll, lay a lettuce leaf horizontally on the bottom half of the moistened rice paper. At the base of the lettuce, place several strands of noodles, 1 teaspoon each of the carrot and cucumber, 2 slices of tofu, 1 tablespoon of bean sprouts, and several mint and cilantro leaves. Be careful not to overstuff the rolls. Lift the bottom edge of the rice paper and carefully place over the noodles and other ingredients, then roll it up once to form a tight cylinder. Fold in the sides of the rice paper and continue to roll the rice paper and filling into a cylinder.

Place the prepared rolls, seam side down, on a platter and cover with a damp kitchen towel. The rolls can be held at room temperature for several hours before serving. Just before serving, cut each roll in half at an angle. Serve with nuoc cham for dipping.

# Summer Panzanella

At its core, panzanella is a toasted-bread salad with a variety of fresh seasonal ingredients and a tangy, vinegary dressing. In the summer, this classic Italian dish is often made with fresh tomatoes, the juice of which is soaked up by the bread. Choose a slightly stale, crusty artisanal bread, and play around with the other ingredients. Try adding sliced cucumber, grated raw zucchini, or baby arugula.

**VINAIGRETTE**

2 tablespoons red wine vinegar

1 tablespoon balsamic vinegar

1 teaspoon Dijon mustard

1 clove garlic, minced

Kosher salt and freshly ground pepper

¼ cup (2 fl oz/60 ml) extra-virgin olive oil

1 tablespoon capers, minced

¼ lb (115 g) green beans

2 large ripe tomatoes

½ cup (2½ oz/70 g) pitted Gaeta olives, halved

¼ lb (115 g) fresh mozzarella, cut into ½-inch (12-mm) dice

⅓ (1 oz/30 g) cup thinly sliced red onion

6 thick slices day-old country bread, crusts removed, lightly toasted

10 fresh mint leaves

5 large fresh basil leaves

Freshly grated Parmesan cheese, for serving

**MAKES 6 SERVINGS**

To make the vinaigrette, in a bowl, whisk together the red wine and balsamic vinegars, mustard, garlic, ¼ teaspoon of salt, and a generous grinding of pepper. Drizzle in the olive oil, whisking constantly until emulsified. Stir in the capers and set aside.

Bring a pot of water to a boil over high heat. Cut the green beans into 1-inch (2.5-cm) lengths and add to the boiling water. Cook until bright green and just tender-crisp, 1–3 minutes. Drain in a colander and place under cold running water to stop the cooking. Drain again and transfer to a large salad bowl.

Cut the tomatoes into bite-size chunks and add to the bowl with the beans. Add the olives, mozzarella, and onion and toss to combine. Tear the bread into pieces and add to the bowl, then chop or tear the mint and basil leaves and scatter over the top. Pour the dressing over the salad and fold gently until all of the ingredients are well coated.

Cover and let the panzanella stand for 1 hour. Just before serving, toss once and garnish with Parmesan.

# Corn, Black Bean & Cherry Tomato Salad with Cilantro-Lime Dressing

Whether a salad or a salsa, you can't go wrong with this Latin-inspired dish. Sweet grilled corn is tossed with tender black beans, cherry tomatoes, and a cilantro-based dressing. This dish makes a terrific side to chile-rubbed grilled chicken, or serve it as a starter with a bowl of tortilla chips.

**CILANTRO-LIME DRESSING**

Juice of 1½ limes

2 tablespoons minced shallot

2 tablespoons minced fresh cilantro

Kosher salt

¼ cup (2 fl oz/60 ml) extra-virgin olive oil

2 large ears corn, shucked

Extra-virgin olive oil, for brushing

2 cans (15 oz/425 g) black beans, drained and rinsed

1 cup (6 oz/170 g) cherry tomatoes, halved

2 ripe avocados, pitted, peeled, and cut into ½-inch (12-mm) pieces

Kosher salt

Fresh cilantro leaves, for garnish

**MAKES 6 SERVINGS**

To make the dressing, in a bowl, whisk together the lime juice, shallot, cilantro, and ¼ teaspoon of salt. Let sit for 5 minutes, then slowly add the oil in a thin stream while whisking.

Prepare a gas or charcoal grill for direct grilling over medium-high heat (400°–450°F/200°–230°C). Brush the grill grate clean.

Brush the corn with oil and grill until charred, about 5 minutes. Transfer to a cutting board. Cut the kernels from the corn and place in a shallow serving bowl. Add the beans and tomatoes.

Drizzle some of the dressing over the salad and toss to combine. Add the avocado, season with salt, and toss gently. Garnish with cilantro. Serve, passing the remaining dressing at the table.

# Farro Salad with Cherry Tomatoes, Arugula & Ricotta Salata

Nutty, tender farro is an ancient wheat cultivated primarily in Tuscany and Umbria. The chewy grains are a natural in salads as they soak up the oil and lemon juice and pair beautifully with other Italian-inspired ingredients, such as tomatoes and ricotta salata. Soaking the farro before cooking ensures that the grains will cook evenly.

1 cup (7¼ oz/205 g) farro

Kosher salt and freshly ground pepper

2 tablespoons extra-virgin olive oil

1 tablespoon fresh lemon juice

1 cup (6 oz/170 g) cherry or grape tomatoes, halved

½ cup (2½ oz/70 g) crumbled ricotta salata or feta cheese

2 green onions, including tender green tops, thinly sliced

¼ cup (½ oz/15 g) shredded fresh basil

**MAKES 4 SERVINGS**

In a large saucepan, combine the farro and 2 qt (1.9 l) water and let stand for 1 hour. Place the pan over medium-high heat, bring to a boil, and add 1 teaspoon of salt. Reduce the heat to medium or medium-low, so the farro simmers steadily, and cook, uncovered, until tender yet still slightly firm and chewy, about 25 minutes. Remove from the heat and drain well in a fine-mesh sieve.

In a serving bowl, whisk together the olive oil and lemon juice until well blended. Whisk in salt and pepper to taste. Add the farro and toss well. Gently stir in the tomatoes, ricotta salata, green onions, and basil until all the ingredients are evenly distributed. Serve at room temperature.

# Summer Pasta Salad with Corn, Olives, Cherry Tomatoes & Feta

This updated pasta salad forgoes the classic mayonnaise-based dressing for a lighter lime-kissed vinaigrette. Fresh grilled corn kernels, briny black olives, sweet cherry tomatoes, and salty feta give the salad texture and balance the flavors of salty, sweet, tangy, and crunchy. Grilled chopped zucchini, roasted peppers, and blanched chopped green beans or sugar snap peas would all be welcome additions.

12 oz (340g) pasta, such as penne or fusilli

2 ears corn, shucked

¼ cup (2 fl oz/60 ml) fresh lime juice

¼ cup (2 fl oz/60 ml) extra-virgin olive oil

¼ cup (½ oz/15 g) minced fresh cilantro or flat-leaf parsley, plus whole leaves for garnish

1½ cups (9 oz/250 g) halved cherry tomatoes, halved

½ cup (2½ oz/70 g) chopped pitted black olives

1 cup (5 oz/140 g) crumbled feta or cubed fresh mozzarella

Kosher salt and freshly ground pepper

**MAKES 6 TO 8 SERVINGS**

Bring a large saucepan of salted water to a boil over high heat. Add the pasta and cook until al dente, about 9 minutes or according to package directions. Drain and rinse well under cold water; drain again and transfer to a large serving bowl.

Prepare a gas or charcoal grill for direct grilling over medium-high heat (400°–450°F/200°–230°C). Brush the grill grate clean.

Place the corn over the heat. Cover the grill and cook, turning occasionally, until nicely grill-marked and crisp-tender, about 5 minutes. Transfer to a cutting board. When cool enough to handle, cut the kernels from the cob.

In a bowl, whisk together the lime juice, oil, and cilantro. Add the corn, tomatoes, and olives to the pasta and toss to combine. Add the lime dressing and toss to combine. Add the feta and season to taste with salt and pepper. Toss again, then garnish with cilantro and serve.

# Shredded Kale Salad with Pancetta & Egg

Hearty kale salad holds up well to bold flavors like salty pancetta, garlic, and balsamic vinegar. To tenderize the kale without cooking it, simply massage it with your hands for a minute or so until the leaves break down slightly and look wilted. Chopped hard-boiled eggs add protein, for a vegan version, omit the egg and pancetta and toss in cooked chickpeas instead.

5 large eggs

2 bunches lacinato kale

Kosher salt and freshly ground pepper

¼ lb (115 g) thick-cut pancetta or bacon, coarsely chopped

3 tablespoons extra-virgin olive oil

1 clove garlic, minced

4 tablespoons (2 fl oz/60 ml) balsamic vinegar

2 tablespoons red wine vinegar

4 tablespoons (½ oz/15 g) fresh flat-leaf parsley leaves

**MAKES 4 SERVINGS**

To hard-boil the eggs, place them in a saucepan just large enough to hold them. Add cold water to cover by 1 inch (2.5 cm) and bring just to a boil over high heat. Remove the pan from the heat and cover with a lid. Let stand for 15 minutes. Prepare a large bowl of ice water. Drain the eggs, then transfer to the ice water and let cool before peeling. Mince the eggs and set aside.

Using a sharp knife, trim the stems from the kale. Roll the leaves up and slice them thinly crosswise, then coarsely chop them. Place the kale in a shallow serving bowl and gently squeeze and massage the leaves with your hands to soften the leaves. Set aside.

In a frying pan over medium heat, cook the pancetta, turning occasionally, until nearly golden, about 5 minutes. (If using bacon, pour off the rendered fat at this point.)

Add 1 tablespoon of the olive oil and the garlic and cook just until the garlic is golden, about 1 minute. Transfer the pancetta and garlic to a small bowl.

Add 2 tablespoons of the balsamic vinegar to the frying pan and cook over medium heat, stirring to scrape up any browned bits on the pan bottom. Pour into a bowl and whisk in the remaining 2 tablespoons of balsamic vinegar, the red wine vinegar, and the remaining 2 tablespoons of olive oil.

Add the pancetta and garlic, 3 tablespoons of the parsley, and ½ teaspoon each salt and pepper to the kale and mix well. Drizzle with the dressing and toss to coat. Add the minced eggs and gently fold them in.

Garnish the mixture with the remaining 1 tablespoon of parsley and serve.

# Heirloom Caprese Salad with Pesto

A simple and popular way to serve fresh tomatoes when they are plentiful, caprese is blissfully versatile. Here, sweet cherry tomatoes and mini fresh mozzarella balls, known as ciliegine, are tossed with basil pesto. The salad is great on its own or heaped onto thick slices of grilled bread. Top or toss with baby arugula if you like.

1 cup (8 fl oz/240 ml) basil pesto, homemade (page 174) or purchased

1½ tablespoons red wine vinegar

¼ cup (2 fl oz/60 ml) extra-virgin olive oil

Kosher salt and freshly ground pepper

4 cups (24 oz/680 g) mixed red, yellow, and orange cherry tomatoes

½ lb (225 g) small fresh mozzarella balls

**MAKES 4 TO 6 SERVINGS**

In a bowl, whisk together the pesto and vinegar. Whisking constantly, slowly add the olive oil until emulsified. Season to taste with salt and pepper.

Slice the cherry tomatoes and mozzarella balls in half, add to the bowl, and toss gently. Season with salt and pepper and mound on a serving platter. Serve at once.

# Grilled Romaine Salad with Anchovy-Mustard Vinaigrette

Grilling lettuce might sound crazy, but romaine holds up well to the smoke and char when left whole. The grill gives the slightly bitter greens a whole new level of flavor, transforming it into a hearty dish that would be perfect alongside a thick, juicy steak. Don't be afraid of using the amount of anchovy called for in the garlicky-mustard vinaigrette—the briny-salty fillets add incredible depth of flavor.

**ANCHOVY-MUSTARD VINAIGRETTE**

1 clove garlic, minced

6 anchovy fillets, minced

1 tablespoon brown mustard

1 large egg yolk

½ cup (4 fl oz/120 ml) extra-virgin olive oil

Juice of 1 lemon

Kosher salt and freshly ground pepper

2 heads romaine lettuce or 3 small heads red-leaf lettuce, loose leaves removed and each head cut lengthwise into quarters

2 tablespoons extra-virgin olive oil

¼ cup (1 oz/30 g) freshly grated Parmesan cheese

**MAKES 4 SERVINGS**

Prepare a gas or charcoal grill for direct and indirect grilling over medium heat (350°–450°F/180°–230°C). Brush the grill grate clean.

To make the vinaigrette, in a salad bowl, combine the garlic and anchovy fillets and mash with the back of a fork until a paste forms. Whisk in the mustard and egg yolk, then whisk in the olive oil, a little at a time, until a thick sauce forms. Stir in the lemon juice and season to taste with salt and pepper. Set aside.

Coat the romaine quarters with the olive oil. Put them on the grate directly over the heat and grill, turning once, just until grill-marked, about 20 seconds per side. Using tongs, move the romaine away from the heat. Coat the romaine with half of the vinaigrette, drizzling it down into the leaves, then sprinkle with half of the cheese. Cover the grill and cook until the cheese just starts to melt and the ends of the lettuce wedges wilt, about 2 minutes.

Transfer the romaine to a platter. Dress with the remaining vinaigrette and a scattering of the remaining cheese. Serve at once.

# Herbed Quinoa with Green Onions, Cucumber & Avocado

Full of protein and fiber, fluffy quinoa is a nutritious addition to any salad. A trio of fresh green onion, parsley, and mint brings vibrant color and a bold flavor to this summery grain salad. Adding pomegranate molasses to the lemony vinaigrette gives it a fragrant sweetness, but if you can't find it you can substitute the same amount of balsamic vinegar.

1½ cups (9 oz/250 g) quinoa

3 cups (24 fl oz/700 ml) low-sodium chicken or vegetable broth

Kosher salt and freshly ground pepper

2 large lemons

2 cloves garlic, minced

1 tablespoon pomegranate molasses

1 teaspoon sugar

½ cup (4 fl oz/120 ml) extra-virgin olive oil

2 large ripe tomatoes, seeded and diced

½ large English cucumber, diced

4 green onions, white and tender green parts, thinly sliced

¼ cup (½ oz/15 g) coarsely chopped fresh flat-leaf parsley

¼ cup (½ oz/15 g) coarsely chopped fresh mint

**MAKES 4 SERVINGS**

Put the quinoa in a fine-mesh strainer, rinse thoroughly under running cold water, and drain. In a saucepan over high heat, bring the broth to a boil. Add the quinoa and ¼ teaspoon of salt, stir once, and reduce the heat to low. Cover and cook, without stirring, until all the water has been absorbed and the grains are tender, about 15 minutes. Fluff the quinoa with a fork and transfer to a large bowl.

Finely grate the zest from 1 of the lemons, then halve both lemons and juice the halves to measure 5 tablespoons. In a small bowl, whisk together the lemon juice and zest, garlic, pomegranate molasses, sugar, ½ teaspoon of salt, and several grindings of pepper until the sugar dissolves. Slowly whisk in the olive oil to make a dressing. Taste and adjust the seasoning, if needed. Add half of the dressing to the quinoa and stir to mix well.

In a small bowl, toss the tomatoes with ¼ teaspoon of salt and let stand until they release their juice, about 5 minutes, then drain in a fine-mesh sieve. Place the cucumber in the small bowl along with the green onions and drizzle with some of the dressing. Toss well, then pour the cucumber mixture over the tomatoes in the sieve to drain. Add the drained tomato-cucumber mixture to the quinoa along with the parsley and mint and stir gently to mix well. Taste and adjust the seasoning, if needed, and serve right away, passing the remaining dressing at the table.

# Shaved Zucchini Salad with Pecorino & Almonds

When your garden is overwhelmed with zucchini and summer squash, this salad makes great use of them. Here, ribbons of zucchini are tenderized with vinaigrette and tossed with salty aged pecorino cheese and toasted nuts. Experiment with other cheeses such as Parmesan, Grana Padano, or aged goat cheese, or nuts such as toasted pine nuts or hazelnuts.

1 tablespoon
balsamic vinegar

1 teaspoon red wine vinegar

Kosher salt and freshly
ground pepper

3 tablespoons extra-virgin
olive oil

2 zucchini and/or
summer squash

Pecorino cheese, for shaving

½ cup (2½ oz/70 g) whole
toasted almonds, chopped

**MAKES 4 TO 6 SERVINGS**

In a large bowl, whisk together the balsamic and red wine vinegars and ¼ teaspoon each of salt and pepper. Add the olive oil in a thin stream, whisking constantly until the vinaigrette is smooth. Set aside.

Using a vegetable peeler, slice the zucchini lengthwise into thin ribbons. Add the zucchini to the bowl with the vinaigrette and toss to coat well. Divide the salad among individual plates. Using the vegetable peeler, shave the cheese over the salads in thin curls. Scatter the toasted almonds over the top and serve.

mains

# Bacon Burgers with Grilled Onions & Roasted Tomato Dressing

These burgers have all the toppings you'd ever want to create the ultimate burger. But burger toppings are personal, so feel free to add or subtract toppings you like or don't like. The most important thing is to choose the best-quality ground beef and to be gentle when preparing the patties so you don't compress the meat.

**GRILLED ONIONS**

2 yellow onions, cut into ¼-inch-thick (6-mm-thick) slices

1 tablespoon extra-virgin olive oil

Kosher salt and freshly ground pepper

½ teaspoon sugar

2 lb (1 kg) ground beef chuck

1 tablespoon Dijon mustard

1 tablespoon Worcestershire sauce

Kosher salt and freshly ground pepper

6 large slices Cheddar or American cheese (optional)

6 hamburger buns, split

Roasted Tomato Dressing (page 176)

12 slices crisp fried bacon

Butter or red leaf lettuce leaves, torn

**MAKES 6 SERVINGS**

To make the onions, prepare a gas or charcoal grill for direct and indirect grilling over medium-high heat (400°–450°F/200°–230°C). Brush the grill grate clean. Brush the onion slices with the olive oil. Put them on the grate directly over the heat and cook, turning once, until deeply grill marked, about 3 minutes per side. Transfer the onion slices to a large piece of aluminum foil and season with ½ teaspoon of salt, ¼ teaspoon of pepper, and the sugar. Fold the foil over the onions, crimp and seal the foil to make a pouch, and put the pouch on the grate away from the heat. Cook until tender, 15–20 minutes. Set aside while you make the burgers.

In a bowl, combine the beef, Dijon, Worcestershire sauce, 1 teaspoon of salt, and ½ teaspoon of pepper and mix with your hands until well blended; do not overmix. Using your hands, gently form the meat into 6 patties no more than 1 inch (2.5 cm) thick.

Place the patties on the grate directly over the heat, cover the grill, and cook for 7 minutes, turning the burgers after about 4 minutes for medium. They should be slightly pink at the center. If you are making cheeseburgers, put cheese slices on each burger 1 minute before the burgers are ready to be removed from the grill.

To toast the buns, place them, cut side down, on the grate over the heat 1 minute before the burgers are ready. Transfer the burgers and buns to a platter, keeping them separate.

To serve, spread the cut sides of the buns with the roasted tomato dressing. Top the bottom bun with a burger patty, then top with the grilled onions, bacon, and lettuce, in that order. Top with the top bun and serve at once.

# Lamb Burger Pitas with Mint-Feta Pesto

Lamb burgers make a nice alternative to an everyday burger, and these are infused with fresh herbs both in the patties and in the lively mint-and-feta pesto. Serve these in thick pita rounds, or opt for a sturdy bun instead. Fresh mint is a strong flavor but is exceptional when paired with lamb. If you like, swap out the pesto for tomato chutney (page 95).

**MINT-FETA PESTO**

1 cup (1 oz/30 g) lightly packed fresh mint leaves

2 tablespoons pine nuts

⅛ teaspoon red pepper flakes

½ cup (4 fl oz/120 ml) extra-virgin olive oil, plus more if needed

1¼ cups (6 oz/170 g) feta cheese, crumbled

Kosher salt and freshly ground pepper

2 tablespoons finely chopped shallot

2 tablespoons minced fresh flat-leaf parsley

1 tablespoon minced fresh mint

1 tablespoon Dijon mustard

2 teaspoons dried rosemary, crushed

1 clove garlic, minced

1½ lb (680 g) ground lamb

½ lb (225 g) ground beef chuck

Kosher salt and freshly ground pepper

6 pita breads

Shredded lettuce for serving

**MAKES 6 SERVINGS**

To make the pesto, in a blender or food processor, combine the mint, pine nuts, and red pepper flakes and pulse until the mint is chopped. With the machine running, slowly add the olive oil in a thin, steady stream, processing until a thin paste forms. If the paste is too thick, add a little more olive oil. Add the feta and pulse 3 or 4 times to mix. Season with salt and pepper. Use right away, or cover and refrigerate for up to 3 days. Bring to room temperature and stir just before serving.

Prepare a gas or charcoal grill for direct grilling over high heat (450°–550°F/ 230°–290°C). Brush the grill grate clean.

In a bowl, mix together the shallot, parsley, mint, mustard, rosemary, and garlic. Using your hands, gently work in the lamb and beef until well blended. Divide the meat mixture into 6 equal portions. Shape each portion into a patty about ¾ inch (2 cm) thick, being careful not to compact the meat too much. Season on both sides with salt and pepper. Make a depression in the center of each patty with your thumb.

Place the patties, indented side up, on the grill directly over the heat and cook, turning once, until nicely charred on both sides, about 5 minutes per side for medium. The patty should give slightly when pressed. During the last 2 minutes of cooking, throw the pita breads onto the edge of the grill and toast lightly, turning once.

Transfer the burgers to a platter. Cut off and discard about one-third of each pita bread and open up the pocket. Place a little of the mint-feta pesto in the bottom of each pita, add a lamb burger, and top with shredded lettuce and a little more pesto. Serve at once.

# Brat Sandwiches with Grilled Peppers & Onions

Beer-braised brats are the adult version of a hot dog and are perfect for a sports-themed event. You can braise the sausages up to 2 hours in advance then cook the sausages, peppers, and onions altogether when everyone is ready for food. Sauerkraut is optional, but it brings a wonderful sharp brininess to these classic sandwiches.

6 cans (12 fl oz/350 ml each) lager-style beer

8 fresh bratwurst sausages

2 yellow onions, coarsely chopped

2 red bell peppers, halved lengthwise and seeded

1 green bell pepper, halved lengthwise and seeded

2 red onions, thickly sliced into rings

Extra-virgin olive oil, for brushing

8 hoagie rolls, split

Whole-grain mustard, for spreading

Sauerkraut for serving (optional)

**MAKES 8 SERVINGS**

In a large pot over high heat, combine the beer, sausages, and yellow onions and bring to a boil. Reduce the heat to medium and simmer gently for about 30 minutes. The brats can sit in this mixture, off the heat, for up to 2 hours.

Prepare a gas or charcoal grill for direct and indirect grilling over medium heat (350°–450°F/180°–230°C). If using charcoal, bank the lit coals on either side (or on one side) of the grill bed, and place a drip pan in the area without coals. If using gas, preheat the burners, then turn off 1 or more of the burners to create a cooler zone. Brush the grill grate clean.

Remove the brats from their beer bath and discard the bath. Drizzle the peppers and red onions with a little olive oil.

Place the brats, bell peppers, and red onions on the grill over the direct heat area and sear, turning occasionally, until nicely grill-marked, about 2 minutes. Move the brats, peppers, and onions to the indirect-heat area and cook, turning frequently, but letting everything get a nice char, about 15 minutes. The vegetables should be tender but not wilted. During the last minute of cooking, place the rolls, cut side down, along the edge of the grill and grill for 1 or 2 minutes until toasted.

Transfer the brats to a large platter and set the rolls to one side. On a cutting board, coarsely chop the red onions and peppers. Spread the cut sides of the rolls with the mustard. Place a brat in each roll and cover with the onion-pepper mixture. Spoon some sauerkraut on top, if using, and serve.

# Grilled Lamb Chops with Herb-Almond Pesto

You can use either lamb rib chops or lamb loin chops in this easy dish; just be sure they are at least 1 inch (2.5 cm) thick so the lamb has time to sear nicely on the outside and remain pink on the inside. The tangy herb and almond pesto beautifully complements the richness of the seared lamb chops.

### HERB-ALMOND PESTO

1½ cups (1½ oz/40 g) lightly packed fresh basil leaves

1 cup (1 oz/30 g) lightly packed fresh flat-leaf parsley leaves

½ cup (½ oz/15 g) lightly packed fresh mint leaves

3 tablespoons slivered almonds, lightly toasted

1 clove garlic, minced

Kosher salt

¾ cup (6 fl oz/180 ml) extra-virgin olive oil

2 teaspoons balsamic vinegar

8 lamb chops, each about 1 inch (2.5 cm) thick

2 tablespoons extra-virgin olive oil

Fine sea salt and freshly ground pepper

**MAKES 4 SERVINGS**

Prepare a gas or charcoal grill for direct grilling over high heat (450°–550°F/230°–290°C). Brush the grill grate clean.

To make the pesto, in a food processor, combine the basil, parsley, mint, almonds, garlic, and ½ teaspoon of salt and process until coarsely chopped, stopping to scrape down the sides of the bowl as needed. With the motor running, drizzle in the olive oil and purée to a thick consistency. Add the vinegar and process to combine. Transfer to a bowl and set aside.

Rub the lamb chops on all sides with the olive oil and season with salt and pepper. Arrange on the grate directly over the heat and grill until seared and nicely grill-marked on the first side, about 3 minutes. Turn and grill on the second side for about 3 minutes longer for medium-rare. Transfer to a platter, tent with aluminum foil, and let rest for 5 minutes.

Arrange 2 chops on each of 4 plates, spoon a generous dollop of pesto on the side, and serve.

# Brined Pork Chops with Bacon-Onion Jam

Thick bone-in pork chops are a popular choice, but they can easily overcook and become dry. Bathing them in brine overnight works wonders on pork, adding moisture and flavor all the way through the meat. Pork chops are terrific with all types of sauces or even grilled fruit (think plums and peaches), but this bacon-onion "jam" is a truly special addition. Serve these with grilled sweet potatoes or a classic potato salad (page 138).

**PORK BRINE**

¼ cup (2 fl oz/60 ml) apple cider vinegar

¼ cup (2 oz/60 g) firmly packed brown sugar

1 teaspoon dried thyme

1 teaspoon juniper berries (optional)

⅛ teaspoon red pepper flakes

Kosher salt and freshly ground black pepper

6 bone-in pork chops, each about 1 inch (2.5 cm) thick

**MAKES 6 SERVINGS**

To make the brine, in a large bowl, combine 6 cups (48 fl oz/1.4 l) water, the vinegar, brown sugar, thyme, juniper berries, if using, red pepper flakes, 2 tablespoons of salt, and 1 tablespoon of pepper and stir until the sugar and salt dissolve. Place the pork chops in a large resealable plastic bag and pour in the brine. Seal the bag, squish the brine around the chops, and refrigerate overnight.

At least 30 minutes before you are ready to begin grilling, remove the chops from the refrigerator. Discard the brine, rinse the chops briefly in cold water, and pat dry with paper towels.

Prepare a gas or charcoal grill for direct and indirect grilling over medium heat (350°–450°F/180°–230°C). If using charcoal, bank the lit coals on either side of the grill bed, leaving a strip in the center without heat. Place a drip pan in the center. If using gas, preheat the burners, then turn off 1 or more of the burners to create a cooler zone. Brush the grill grate clean.

**BACON-ONION JAM**

6 slices thick-cut
applewood-smoked bacon

1 cup (4 oz/115 g) chopped
yellow onion

2 tablespoons unsalted butter

½ cup (4 fl oz/120 ml)
reduced-sodium
chicken broth

1 tablespoon
whole-grain mustard

1 fresh thyme sprig

Kosher salt and freshly
ground pepper

While the grill heats, make the jam, in a frying pan over medium heat, fry the bacon until crisp, about 5 minutes. Transfer the bacon to paper towels to drain, then chop finely and set aside. Discard all but 3 tablespoons of the fat from the pan and add the onion to the fat. Cook over medium heat, stirring, until caramelized, about 15 minutes. Add the butter and cook until melted, then add the broth, mustard, and thyme. Cook until the mixture thickens, about 15 minutes. Stir in the bacon and season with salt and pepper. Set aside until ready to use, or cover and refrigerate for up to 4 days; bring to room temperature before serving.

Place the pork chops on the grill over the direct heat and sear, turning once, until nicely grill-marked on both sides, 2–3 minutes on each side. Move the chops to the indirect heat area, cover the grill, and cook until the chops are somewhat firm to the touch, about 15 minutes for medium, or until an instant-read thermometer inserted horizontally into the center of a chop away from the bone registers 145°F (63°C).

Transfer the chops to a platter and let rest for 10 minutes. Serve the pork chops with the bacon-onion jam on the side.

# Carne Asada Tacos with Smoky Tomato Salsa

Marinating skirt steak overnight permeates the meat with cumin, coriander, garlic, and lime. Make sure your grill is hot so the steak sears quickly on the outside, creating a nicely charred crust. Cook the steak to medium-rare or medium for the best results since rare skirt steak can be chewy and tough. You only need tortillas, some salsa, and a few slices of avocado for the perfect carne asada taco.

1 tablespoon ground cumin

1 teaspoon ground coriander

Kosher salt and freshly ground pepper

1 skirt steak, about 2 lb (1 kg)

1 lime, halved, plus lime wedges for serving

4 cloves garlic, coarsely chopped

2 tablespoons chopped fresh cilantro

Extra-virgin olive oil, for brushing

24 corn tortillas, 6 inches (15 cm) in diameter

Smoky Tomato Salsa (page 176) or your favorite salsa, for serving

2 avocados, pitted, peeled, and sliced

**MAKES 6 SERVINGS**

In a small bowl, mix together the cumin, coriander, 1 teaspoon of salt, and 1 teaspoon of pepper. Sprinkle the steak evenly on both sides with the spice mixture, then squeeze half a lime over each side. Rub the garlic and cilantro into both sides of the steak. Place the steak in a large resealable plastic bag, seal the bag, and refrigerate overnight.

At least 30 minutes before you are ready to begin grilling, remove the steak from the refrigerator. Brush the steak on both sides with olive oil.

Prepare a gas or charcoal grill for direct grilling over high heat (450°–550°F/230°–290°C). Brush the grill grate clean.

Place the steak on the grill directly over the heat and cook, turning once, until nicely charred on both sides and fairly firm to the touch, about 4 minutes per side for medium-rare or 6 minutes per side for medium. (Rare skirt steak can be a little tough. Medium-rare or medium works best.) Transfer the steak to a cutting board and let rest for 5 minutes. Meanwhile, warm the tortillas on the grill, about 1 minute on each side, then stack and wrap them in a kitchen towel.

Thinly slice the steak against the grain. To assemble each taco, overlap 2 tortillas, top with the meat, add a spoonful of the salsa, and 1 or 2 slices of avocado. Add a lime wedge to each plate. Fold the tortillas around the filling and serve.

# Tacos Al Pastor with Grilled Pineapple & Onions

The key to al pastor, meaning "shepherd style," is the adobada marinade featuring achiote paste, a deep red paste that combines red-hued annatto seed and spices. Tacos al pastor are a popular street food in Mexico, where the meat is spit-grilled in similar fashion to shawarma. Here the marinated pork is cooked on a hot grill and served with the requisite pineapple and onion.

2 oz (60 g) achiote paste

2 small chipotle chiles in adobo sauce, minced

½ cup (4 fl oz/120 ml) fresh orange juice

¼ cup (2 fl oz/60 ml) plus 1 tablespoon avocado or canola oil

Kosher salt and freshly ground pepper

2 lb (1 kg) pork loin, cut into ¼-inch (6-mm) slices

½ pineapple, peeled, cored, and cut into ½-inch (12-mm) rings

1 red onion, cut into ½-inch (12-mm) slices

12 corn or flour tortillas, warmed

Chopped fresh cilantro, for serving

**MAKES 6 SERVINGS**

In a blender, combine the achiote paste, chipotle chiles, orange juice, ¼ cup (2 fl oz/ 60 ml) of avocado oil, and ½ teaspoon of salt and process to a smooth purée. Transfer to a nonreactive bowl, add the pork, and toss to coat thoroughly. Cover and let marinate in the refrigerator for 1–4 hours.

Prepare a gas or charcoal grill for direct and indirect grilling over medium-high heat (400°–450°F/200°–230°C). If using a charcoal grill, move the hot coals to one side of the grill. If you are using a gas grill, turn off the middle set of flames when you are ready to grill. Brush the grill grate clean.

Brush the pineapple and onion on both sides with the remaining 1 tablespoon of avocado oil and season with salt and pepper. Arrange the pineapple and onion on the grate directly over the heat and grill, turning once, until soft and nicely grill-marked, about 4 minutes per side. Using tongs, move to the cooler area of the grill and let them continue to soften and caramelize while you cook the pork.

Remove the pork from the marinade and discard the marinade. Arrange the pork on the grate directly over the heat and grill, turning once, until opaque throughout, about 2 minutes per side. Transfer the pork, pineapple, and onion to a cutting board. Let cool slightly, then chop into bite-size pieces. To assemble, fill the tortillas with pork, pineapple, and onion, dividing them evenly. Top with the cilantro, then serve right away.

# North Carolina–Style Pulled Pork Sandwiches with Slaw

Pulled pork is great in just about anything, from tacos and nachos to sandwiches—it's even terrific for topping a salad. Don't forget to rub the pork shoulder with the spice rub and leave it overnight, uncovered, in the refrigerator—it helps dry the exterior so the pork will soak up the flavor of the smoke more readily. The pork takes time to transform itself into meltingly tender pieces, but much of it is hands-off.

Basic Barbecue Rub
(page 175)

1 bone-in pork shoulder
roast, 6–7 lb (2.7–3.2 kg)

Western Carolina Barbecue
Sauce (page 175)

About 20 large handfuls
wood chips or chunks

About 12 burger buns, split

Creamy Coleslaw (page 131)

**MAKES 10 TO
12 SERVINGS**

Set a large wire rack on a rimmed baking sheet. Scatter the rub evenly over the pork, patting it in with your fingers. If you have any rub left over, mix it into the sauce. Place the pork on the rack in the pan and refrigerate, uncovered, overnight.

Prepare a gas or charcoal grill for direct and indirect grilling over very low heat (225°–250°F/110°–120°C), or heat a smoker to 225°F (110°C). If using charcoal, wrap the wood chips in several perforated aluminum foil packets and place one packet on the hot coals, or place a handful of wood chunks directly on the coals. If using a gas grill, wrap the chips in several perforated foil packets and put one packet directly over one of the gas burners under the cooking grate. Or if your grill has a smoker box, use it.

Brush the grill grate clean. Place an aluminum foil pan of hot water on the grate on the heated side of the grill. Put the pork, fatty side up, on the grate over the unheated side of the grill. Cover and cook until the pork is dark all over and fall-apart tender and an instant-read thermometer inserted into the thickest part away from bone registers about 190°F (87°C), 4–5 hours total. If you are using charcoal, you will need to replace the coals about once an hour during cooking. Refill the water pan with hot water as needed to keep the pan from going dry. If your grill has a temperature gauge, it should stay between 225°–250°F/110°–120°C. Whenever the wood stops smoking, add another foil packet of chips or handful of chunks.

Transfer the meat to a cutting board and let rest for 20 minutes to allow the juices to redistribute. Using tongs and a knife, pull and/or chop the pork into shreds, breaking up crispy bits and discarding bones and excess fat. Put the shredded pork in a large disposable aluminum pan, add about 2 cups of the sauce, and stir to mix evenly. Drizzle on more sauce to taste.

Mound the pork on the bun bottoms, top with some barbecue sauce and slaw, then cover with the bun tops and serve at once.

# Grilled Pork Belly Wraps with Korean Ssamjang

Braising pork belly in the oven for a few hours helps render some of the fat, allowing you achieve a crispy exterior on the grill. Here, pork belly is glazed with Korean ssamjang sauce—a mixture of doenjang and gochujang, garlic, green onions, honey, and sesame. It is served wrapped in lettuce leaves with sticky rice and more of the spicy-sweet ssamjang sauce. Sticky rice, doenjang, and gochujang can be found in Asian markets.

1½ lb (680 g) center-cut pork belly

Coarse sea salt

1½ cups (12 fl oz/350 ml) unseasoned rice vinegar

**SSAMJANG SAUCE**

⅓ cup (3 oz/90 g) doenjang (Korean fermented soybean paste)

1 tablespoon gochujang (Korean red chile paste)

1 large clove garlic, minced

2 green onions, white and pale green parts, chopped

3 teaspoons honey

2 teaspoons toasted sesame oil

2 teaspoons sesame seeds, toasted

2 cups (11 oz/310 g) cooked sweet glutinous (sticky) rice

2 tablespoons seasoned rice vinegar

1 head butter lettuce, separated into leaves

Kimchi, for serving (optional)

**MAKES 4 SERVINGS**

Preheat the oven to 300°F (150°C). Rub the pork belly all over with 3 tablespoons of salt and set the pork, fat side up, in a baking dish just a little bigger than the pork itself. Add the vinegar to the baking dish; it should come about halfway up the sides of the pork. Cover the baking dish tightly with aluminum foil and braise the pork in the oven for 3 hours.

To make the sauce, in a small bowl, combine all of the ingredients and mix well. Set aside, or store in an airtight container in the refrigerator for up to 1 week.

Remove the pork from the oven and let cool, still covered, to room temperature. When cooled, uncover the baking dish and peel off and discard the skin and the top layer of fat that comes off with the skin. Cut the pork into bricks about 2 inches (5 cm) long and 1 inch (2.5 cm) wide.

Prepare a gas or charcoal grill for direct grilling over medium-high heat (400°–450°F/200°–230°C). Brush the grill grate clean.

Place the pork belly on the grate, meat side down, and sear on all sides, 2–3 minutes per side, including the ends. Grill the fatty side last. During the last few minutes, brush the bricks all over with the ssamjang sauce. Transfer the pork to a plate.

Put the rice in a serving bowl, add the seasoned rice vinegar, and stir and toss to mix evenly. Invite your guests to wrap the pork belly bricks in lettuce leaves with a little rice, more ssamjang, and some kimchi, if using.

# Grilled Pizza with Prosciutto & Hot-Pepper Honey

Salty prosciutto drizzled with honey and hot-pepper sauce is a satisfying and unexpected combination for topping grilled pizzas. Make sure to grill one side of the pizza first to give it more structure. You can also use a grill-safe pizza stone to cook the pizzas, just heat it on the grill first before adding the topped pizza. A handful of arugula is a nice addition to these pizzas as well.

¼ cup (3 oz/90 g) honey

2 teaspoons hot-pepper sauce

¼ teaspoon red pepper flakes

Extra-virgin olive oil, for brushing

1 lb (450 g) pizza dough, homemade (page 174) or purchased

1 cup (8 fl oz/240 ml) Pizza Sauce (page 174)

¾ lb (340 g) fresh mozzarella cheese, thinly sliced

2 oz (60 g) prosciutto, sliced paper-thin

**MAKES 4 PIZZAS**

Prepare a gas or charcoal grill for direct grilling over medium heat on one side (350°–450°F/180°–230°C) and low heat (about 300°F/150°) on the other side. Brush the grill grate clean.

In a small bowl, stir together the honey, hot-pepper sauce, and red pepper flakes.

Brush four 12-inch (30-cm) squares of aluminum foil on one side with olive oil. Cut the dough into 4 equal pieces. Put a piece of the dough in the center of a piece of foil and press and stretch the dough into a 10-inch (25-cm) round about ⅛ inch (3 mm) thick. Brush the top of the dough with olive oil. Repeat with the remaining dough and foil squares.

One at a time, invert each round of dough directly onto the hotter side of the grill. Using tongs and a spatula, peel the foil carefully off the dough. Grill until the dough is nicely browned on the bottom and almost dry on top, 1–2 minutes. After about 1 minute, use the tongs and the spatula to rotate the dough 90 degrees to prevent burning. Repeat with all the dough rounds.

Transfer the grilled dough rounds to a cutting board, with the grilled sides up. Spread ¼ (2 fl oz/60 ml) cup sauce on each round. Arrange the mozzarella and then the prosciutto over the sauce, dividing them evenly among the rounds. One at a time, lift the pizzas and place them back on the grill over the cooler side. Cover the grill and cook, rotating each round about 90 degrees halfway through the cooking, until the bottoms brown and the cheese melts, about 5 minutes.

Using a large spatula and tongs, transfer the pizzas to the cutting board and drizzle the hot-pepper honey evenly over the tops. Cut each pizza into 4 wedges and serve.

# Pork Bánh Mì Burgers with Pickled Vegetables

The flavors of authentic Vietnamese bánh mì sandwiches are re-created here in these easy-to-make pork burgers. A little sugar added to the patties helps caramelize the burger, and the fish sauce gives it amazing flavor. If you like, omit the baguette and serve the burgers, pickled vegetables, and fried egg over steamed rice for a delicious burger bowl.

1 carrot, shredded

½ small red onion, halved and thinly sliced

3½ teaspoons sugar

Kosher salt and freshly ground pepper

¼ cup (2 fl oz/60 ml) rice vinegar

½ cup (4 fl oz/120 ml) mayonnaise

2½ tablespoons sriracha

1½ tablespoons fresh lemon juice

1 lb (450 g) ground pork

4 fresh basil leaves, chopped

2 green onions, white and tender green parts only, minced

1½ tablespoons fish sauce

4 teaspoons avocado or canola oil

4 large eggs

½ cup (½ oz/15 g) lightly packed fresh cilantro leaves

1 baguette

**MAKES 4 SERVINGS**

In a small bowl, combine the carrot and red onion. Add 1½ teaspoons of the sugar, ½ teaspoon of salt, the vinegar, and 3 tablespoons water and stir to combine. Let stand at room temperature.

In another small bowl, stir together the mayonnaise, sriracha, and lemon juice. Let stand at room temperature.

In a large bowl, combine the pork, basil, green onions, fish sauce, and the remaining 2 teaspoons of sugar. Using your hands, form the mixture into 4 rectangular patties. Season both sides well with salt and pepper. Warm 2 teaspoons of the avocado oil in a nonstick frying pan over medium heat. Add the patties and cook, turning once, until medium, 5–6 minutes per side. Transfer to a plate and cover to keep warm.

In the same frying pan over medium heat, warm the remaining 2 teaspoons of avocado oil. Fry the eggs until set but still runny, 5–6 minutes.

While the eggs are cooking, drain the liquid from the vegetables and stir in the cilantro. Slice the baguette into four 4½-inch (11½-cm) lengths and split each one open. Slather the cut sides of the baguette with the sriracha mayo. Set the burgers on the baguettes and top with the pickled vegetables and fried eggs. Close the burgers and serve right away.

# Korean Short Ribs

Sweet, salty, hot, and tangy flavors infuse these thin-cut grilled Korean-style ribs. Be sure to marinate the ribs overnight, which makes cooking them the next day effortless. Ask your butcher for flanken-cut ribs, which are cut across the bone and thinner than the thicker bone-in English cut ribs. The marinade and sauce are great on chicken or pork, too.

**MARINADE**

½ cup (4 fl oz/120 ml) reduced-sodium soy sauce

¼ cup (2 oz/60 g) firmly packed light brown sugar

2 tablespoons rice vinegar

2 tablespoons toasted sesame oil

2 tablespoons minced garlic

1 tablespoon minced peeled fresh ginger

1 tablespoon ketchup, store-bought or homemade (page 176)

1 teaspoon red pepper flakes

5 lb (2.3 kg) flanken-cut beef short ribs, prepared by your butcher

**MAKES 6 SERVINGS**

To make the marinade, in a large bowl, combine the soy sauce, brown sugar, vinegar, sesame oil, garlic, ginger, ketchup, and red pepper flakes and whisk to dissolve the sugar. Place the ribs in a large resealable plastic bag and pour in the marinade. Seal the bag, squish the marinade around the ribs, and refrigerate overnight. Be sure to turn the bag over several times while the ribs are marinating.

Prepare a gas or charcoal grill for direct grilling over high heat (450°–550°F/230°–290°C). Brush the grill grate clean.

Remove the ribs from the marinade and discard the marinade. Pat the ribs dry with paper towels. Place the ribs on the grill directly over the heat and cook, turning once, until medium, 6–8 minutes total. Transfer the ribs to a platter and let rest for 5–10 minutes. Serve at once.

# Baby Back Ribs with Spicy-Sweet Glaze

Smoke-kissed baby back ribs are one of the ultimate grilling achievements. This method gently bakes the ribs for an hour in the oven before they are finished on the grill, reducing the amount of hands-on grill time and ensuring the ribs stay tender. This spicy-sweet glaze is a terrific partner to pork, but you can use this same method with your favorite barbecue sauce instead of the glaze for a more classic version.

**SPICY-SWEET GLAZE**

⅔ cup (6 oz/170 g) ketchup, store-bought or homemade (page 176)

⅔ cup (3 fl oz/90 ml) fresh orange juice

3 tablespoons black bean–garlic sauce

2 tablespoons chile-garlic sauce

2 tablespoons finely grated peeled fresh ginger

2 tablespoons dry sherry

2 tablespoons firmly packed light brown sugar

1 tablespoon granulated sugar

1 tablespoon toasted sesame oil

1 tablespoon tamari or reduced-sodium soy sauce

¼ cup (1¼ oz/35 g) Dijon mustard

2 racks baby back ribs, each about 3 lb (1.4 kg), silverskin removed

¼ cup (2 oz/60 g) firmly packed light brown sugar

Kosher salt and freshly ground pepper

About 2 cups wood chips, soaked in water for 30 minutes

**MAKES 4 SERVINGS**

To make the glaze, stir together all of the ingredients until well mixed. Set aside or refrigerate in an airtight container for up to 3 days.

Preheat the oven to 250°F (120°C). Brush the mustard on both sides of the racks and sprinkle evenly with the brown sugar, 1 tablespoon of salt, and 1 tablespoon of pepper. Gently pat the sugar, salt, and pepper into the mustard. Place the ribs, side by side, on a large piece of aluminum foil and loosely wrap the ribs. Set on a rimmed baking sheet. Bake the ribs in the oven for 1 hour.

Prepare a gas or charcoal grill for direct and indirect grilling over very low heat (225°–250°F/110°–120°C). If using charcoal, bank the lit coals on either side of the grill bed, leaving a strip in the center without heat. Place a drip pan in the center strip and fill the pan with water. Add about 1 cup of the wood chips to the fire just before grilling. If using gas, fill the smoker box with about 1 cup of the wood chips, then preheat the grill. Turn off 1 or more burners to create a cooler zone. Brush and oil the grill grate. Brush the grill grate clean.

Remove the ribs from the oven. Unwrap the ribs and discard the foil. Place the ribs over the indirect heat area of the grill, cover the grill, and smoke for 1 hour, adding the remaining wood chips after about 30 minutes.

If using a charcoal grill, ready some coals to raise the temperature of the fire to medium, then uncover the grill and add the hot coals. If using a gas grill, uncover the grill and raise the heat to medium. Move the ribs, meat side down, to the direct heat area of the grill and brush with the glaze. Cook for 5 minutes, then turn the ribs and brush the bone side with glaze. Continue to cook for 20 minutes, turning and basting with the glaze every 5 minutes.

Transfer the racks to a cutting board and let rest for about 10 minutes. Cut the racks into individual ribs, pile them on a platter, and serve at once with the remaining glaze.

# Smoked St. Louis Ribs with Peach Bourbon Barbecue Sauce

St. Louis–style ribs are thicker and meatier than baby back ribs, and they are cut from the belly side of the rib cage, underneath the back ribs. They contain more fat, which means they also stay tender when smoked. Peach nectar in the homemade barbecue sauce brings sweet Southern aromas to this dish, but you can also use any favorite barbecue sauce you like.

Basic Barbecue Rub
(page 175)

1 teaspoon ancho
chile powder

1 teaspoon chipotle
chile powder

1 teaspoon granulated garlic

2 racks St. Louis–style pork
spareribs, each about 2 lb
(1 kg), silverskin removed

About 12 large handfuls
wood chips or chunks

Peach Bourbon Barbecue
Sauce (page 175)

**MAKES 4 TO 6 SERVINGS**

In a small bowl, stir together the rub, ancho and chipotle chile powders, and garlic, mixing well. Generously coat the ribs all over with the seasoning mixture. Wrap the slabs in plastic wrap and refrigerate for at least 8 hours or up to 12 hours.

Prepare a gas or charcoal grill for direct and indirect grilling over very low heat (225°–270°F/110°–135°C), or heat a smoker to 250°F (120°C). If using charcoal, wrap the wood chips in several perforated aluminum foil packets and place one packet on the hot coals, or place a handful of wood chunks directly on the coals. If using a gas grill, wrap the chips in several perforated foil packets and put one packet directly over one of the gas burners under the cooking grate. Or if your grill has a smoker box, use it.

Brush the grill grate clean. Place an aluminum foil pan of hot water on the grate on the heated side of the grill. Put the ribs, meaty side down, on the grate away from the heat. If you have a rib rack, stand the ribs in the rack. Cover the grill and cook the ribs, rotating them 180 degrees once or twice for even cooking, until they are tender and the meat starts to pull back from the ends of the bones, 2–2½ hours. If you are using charcoal, you will need to replace the coals about once an hour during cooking. Whenever the wood stops smoking, add another foil packet of chips or handful of chunks. Refill the water pan with hot water as needed to keep the pan from going dry. If your grill has a temperature gauge, it should stay around 275°F (135°C).

During the last 15 minutes, brush the ribs with some of the sauce every 5 minutes or so. If cooking directly on the grill rather than with a rib rack, brush the bone side of the ribs with the sauce and then turn and cook that side until lightly browned. Brush the meat side and then turn and cook that side until lightly browned. Continue brushing and cooking until the ribs are nicely glazed with sauce and the meat side is face up.

Transfer the ribs to a platter and let rest for 10–20 minutes. Cut the ribs into 3- to 4-bone servings or cut into individual ribs. Serve with the remaining sauce on the side.

# Bone-In Rib Eyes with Chimichurri & Grilled Corn Salad

This all-in-one meal is the epitome of summer indulgence, when corn and tomtoes are at their peak. For an impressive presentation, choose bone-in rib eyes with a long bone, aka the cowboy or tomahawk steak. Large steaks can be divided between two or more people if you like. And don't forget the herb-filled chimichurri sauce—it adds tons of flavor to the beef and pairs nicely with a corn and cherry tomato salad.

**DIJON VINAIGRETTE**

3 tablespoons Dijon mustard

3 tablespoons apple cider vinegar

Juice of ½ lemon

1 teaspoon chopped garlic

1 teaspoon chopped shallot

½ teaspoon sugar

¼ teaspoon cracked yellow mustard seeds

½ cup (4 fl oz/120 ml) extra-virgin olive oil

4 bone-in rib-eye steaks, preferably long bone, each about 1½ inches (4 cm) thick

Kosher salt and freshly ground pepper

4 ears fresh corn, shucked

2 cups (2 oz/60 g) baby arugula

1 cup (6 oz/170 g) cherry tomatoes, halved

2 tablespoons chopped fresh flat-leaf parsley

Chimichurri (page 176)

**MAKES 4 SERVINGS**

To make the vinaigrette, in a blender or food processor, combine the mustard, vinegar, lemon juice, garlic, shallot, sugar, and mustard seeds. Pulse briefly to mix. With the motor running, slowly add the olive oil and process until the mixture emulsifies. Set aside until ready to use.

At least 30 minutes before you are ready to begin grilling, remove the steaks from the refrigerator. Season both sides of the steaks generously with salt and pepper.

Prepare a gas or charcoal grill for direct grilling over medium-high heat on one side (400°–450°F/200°C–230°C) and high heat on the other side (450°–550°F/230°–290°C). Brush the grill grate clean.

Place the corn ears on the grill over the medium-high heat and cook, turning every couple of minutes, until they are lightly charred all the way around and the kernels are tender, 5–7 minutes. Let cool while you grill the steaks.

Place the steaks on the hottest part of the grill and cook for 4 minutes. Using tongs or a wide spatula, rotate each steak a quarter turn (90 degrees), and continue cooking for another 3 minutes, then turn the steaks. Cook the steaks until well marked and cooked to your liking, about another 5 minutes for medium-rare, or until an instant-read thermometer inserted into the center of a steak away from the bone registers 135°F (57°C). If you want to cook the steaks to medium, find a cool spot along the edge of the charcoal grill or turn the burners down on the gas grill to medium heat.

Transfer the steaks to warmed plates and let rest for 5–10 minutes. Holding each ear of corn, stem end down, on a cutting board, cut off the kernels with a sharp knife. Transfer the kernels to a bowl. Pour some of the vinaigrette over the corn, add the arugula, tomatoes, and parsley and toss well.

Serve the steaks drizzled with the chimichurri and the salad alongside.

# Texas-Style Barbecue Brisket

Making a home-smoked brisket is an endeavor that is probably only for the most committed to the barbecue arts. It takes a long time to cook, and you must closely watch the grill, but the results are incredible. This is the meal to make when you have a big crowd to feed and want to impress your family and friends, or if you just want a project. Be sure to start very early in the morning, because the brisket will take at least 12 hours to cook until it is beautifully tender.

1 beef brisket, about 5 lb (2.3 kg), fat trimmed to ½ inch (12 mm)

Kosher salt and freshly ground pepper

1 tablespoon granulated garlic

About 8 cups wood chips, preferably hickory or mesquite, soaked in water for 30 minutes

Classic Barbecue Sauce (page 175), or your favorite purchased barbecue sauce

**MAKES 10 TO 12 SERVINGS**

At least 1 hour before you are ready to begin cooking, remove the brisket from the refrigerator. Season the brisket generously all over with salt and pepper. Sprinkle the garlic evenly over the brisket, then gently rub it into the surface.

Prepare a gas or charcoal grill for direct and indirect grilling over very low heat (225°–250°F/110°–120°C), or heat a smoker to 225°F (110°C). If using charcoal, bank the lit coals on either side of the grill bed, leaving a strip in the center without heat. Place a drip pan in the center strip and fill the pan with water. Add about 2 cups of the wood chips to the fire just before grilling. If using gas, fill the smoker box with up to 2 cups of the wood chips, then preheat the grill. Turn off 1 or more of the burners to create a cooler zone. Brush the grill grate clean.

Place the brisket on the grill over the indirect heat area and cover the grill. Smoke the meat for about 4 hours, adding additional wood chips every 30 minutes or so and more coals as needed if using charcoal.

Remove the brisket from the grill and wrap it in aluminum foil. Return the brisket to the smoker or grill and cook it slowly for another 4–6 hours, or place in a roasting pan and slow-roast in a 250°F (120°C) oven for an additional 4–6 hours. The brisket is ready when it is fork-tender.

Transfer the brisket to a cutting board and let rest for 30 minutes–1 hour. Remove the foil, thinly slice against the grain and arrange the slices on a platter. Serve with the barbecue sauce—reheated or at room temperature—on the side.

# Orange Mojo Pork Tenderloin

Mojo is a Cuban marinade and sauce made from citrus juices and garlic and a handful of other ingredients. This recipe is easy enough for a midweek meal, especially if you marinate the pork the night before, and special enough for a dinner party. The marinade is equally terrific on chicken and shrimp. Serve the pork with steamed rice, black beans, and fried plantains.

**ORANGE MOJO**

2 tablespoons cumin seeds

1½ cups (12 fl oz/350 ml) extra-virgin olive oil

2–4 jalapeño chiles, seeded and minced

12 cloves garlic, minced

Kosher salt and freshly ground pepper

¾ cup (6 fl oz/180 ml) fresh orange juice

¼ cup (½ oz/15 g) chopped fresh cilantro

¼ cup (½ oz/15 g) chopped fresh oregano

3 tablespoons sherry

2 teaspoons ground cumin

½ teaspoon ground coriander

Kosher salt and freshly ground pepper

2 pork tenderloins, each 1½–2 lb (680 g–1 kg), silverskin removed

**MAKES 4 TO 6 SERVINGS**

To make the mojo, in a frying pan over medium heat, toast the cumin seeds, shaking the pan often, until aromatic, about 30 seconds. Add the olive oil and heat until warm. Add the jalapeños, garlic, and 1 teaspoon each of salt and pepper and heat for 3–5 minutes to blend the flavors. Remove from the heat.

In a blender, combine the orange juice, cilantro, oregano, and sherry. Pour in the warm oil mixture and blend until smooth. You should have about 2¾ cups. Divide the mixture in half and let cool. (The mojo can be made in advance and refrigerated for up to 2 days. Bring to room temperature before using.)

In a small bowl, mix together the cumin, coriander, 1 teaspoon of salt, and ½ teaspoon of pepper. Rub the pork tenderloins evenly with the spice mixture. Place the pork tenderloins in a large resealable plastic bag and pour in half of the mojo. Seal the bag, squish the marinade around the tenderloins, and refrigerate for at least 4 hours or up to overnight.

At least 30 minutes before you are ready to begin grilling, remove the pork from the refrigerator. Discard the marinade and lightly pat the tenderloins dry with paper towels.

Prepare a gas or charcoal grill for direct grilling over medium heat (350°–450°F/ 180°–230°C). Brush the grill grate clean.

Place the tenderloins on the grill directly over the heat and cook until nicely grill-marked, 3–4 minutes. Roll them about one-quarter turn and cook for another 3–4 minutes. Continue to roll and cook in this manner for a total of about 15 minutes for medium. The pork is ready when it feels fairly firm to the touch, or when an instant-read thermometer inserted into the thickest part registers 145°F (63°C). The internal temperature of the tenderloins will rise a few degrees as they rest.

Transfer the tenderloins to a cutting board and let rest for about 5 minutes. Slice on the diagonal against the grain and arrange the slices on a platter. Serve at once with the remaining mojo sauce.

# Chipotle Barbecued Chicken

Brining chicken pieces before grilling them is a tried-and-tested method that not only keeps meat moist but also helps flavor it all the way through. The best bet for barbecued chicken is chicken that is on the bone, rather than boneless. If you don't want to use a whole bird, purchase 4 to 6 large bone-in chicken thighs instead.

**POULTRY BRINE**

5 tablespoons (2 oz/60 g) kosher salt

2 tablespoons dried basil

2 tablespoons coriander seeds

1 tablespoon peppercorns

1 tablespoon yellow mustard seeds

1 teaspoon granulated garlic

2 bay leaves

1 whole chicken, about 4 lb (1.8 kg), neck and giblets removed, cut into 4 or 6 pieces

2 cups (16 fl oz/475 ml) Classic Barbecue Sauce (page 175) or your favorite barbecue sauce

**MAKES 4 TO 6 SERVINGS**

To make the brine, in a large bowl, combine 2 qt (1.9 l) water, the salt, basil, coriander, peppercorns, mustard seeds, garlic, and bay leaves and stir until the salt dissolves. Put the chicken pieces in a large resealable plastic bag and pour in the brine. Seal the bag, squish the brine around the chicken, and refrigerate overnight.

At least 30 minutes before you are ready to begin grilling, remove the chicken from the brine and discard the brine. Rinse the chicken pieces briefly and pat dry with paper towels.

Prepare a gas or charcoal grill for direct and indirect grilling over medium heat (350°–450°F/180°–230°C). If using charcoal, bank the lit coals on either side of the grill bed, leaving a strip in the center without heat. Place a drip pan in the center. If using gas, preheat the burners, then turn off 1 or more of the burners to create a cooler zone. Brush the grill grate clean.

Place the chicken pieces on the grill over the direct heat area and sear, turning once, for 2 minutes on each side. Move the chicken pieces to the indirect heat area, cover the grill, and cook for 30 minutes. Start brushing the chicken with the barbecue sauce, turning and brushing the pieces every 5 minutes, for about 15 minutes longer. The chicken is ready when it is firm to the touch and the juices run clear when a thigh or breast is pierced with a knife tip.

Transfer the chicken pieces to a platter and serve at once. Pass the remaining sauce at the table.

# Chicken Shawarma Naan Tacos

This brilliant mash-up dish merges Middle Eastern spiced chicken breasts, tender naan, garlicky yogurt-tahini sauce, and fresh salad for a whole new take on a taco. The chicken and onions are seared in a hot cast-iron pan, but they can also be grilled. If you can't find mini naan, tuck the chicken and vegetables into toasted pita halves.

**YOGURT-TAHINI SAUCE**

¾ cup (6 oz/170 g) plain whole-milk yogurt

1 clove garlic, minced

2 tablespoons tahini

1 tablespoon minced fresh cilantro

1 tablespoon fresh lemon juice

Kosher salt and freshly ground pepper

2 tablespoons extra-virgin olive oil

2 teaspoons curry powder

1 teaspoon ground cumin

2 cloves garlic, minced

Juice of ½ lemon

4 boneless, skinless chicken breasts, about 2 lb (1 kg) total, thinly sliced

Kosher salt and freshly ground pepper

1 red onion, halved and cut into ½-inch (12-mm) slices

8 mini naan breads, toasted

2 cups (3½ oz/100 g) shredded romaine lettuce

2 ripe plum tomatoes, chopped

**MAKES 4 TO 8 SERVINGS**

To make the sauce, in a bowl, stir together the yogurt, garlic, tahini, cilantro, and lemon juice. Season with salt and pepper.

In a bowl, stir together 1 tablespoon of the olive oil, the curry, cumin, garlic, and lemon juice. Add the chicken, season well with salt and pepper, and toss to coat thoroughly. Let stand at room temperature for 20 minutes.

In a small bowl, toss the onion with the remaining 1 tablespoon of olive oil and season with salt and pepper.

Heat a large cast-iron frying pan over high heat. When the pan is really hot, add the onion and cook, turning occasionally, until nicely browned all over, about 6 minutes. Transfer to a plate and cover to keep warm. Do not wipe the pan clean.

Add the chicken to the pan and cook, turning once, until opaque throughout and lightly browned on both sides, about 3 minutes per side.

To assemble, top the naan with the grilled chicken and onions, dividing evenly. Top the chicken with the lettuce and tomato, dividing evenly, then generously drizzle the tahini sauce over each portion. Fold over and serve right away.

# Tandoori Chicken Kebabs with Tomato Chutney

This rendition of chicken skewers marinated in fragrant Indian spices is sure to be a crowd-pleaser. Make the sweet-tart tomato chutney in advance so it has an opportunity to sit and soap up all the subtle spices. You can also use purchased chutney, such as a fresh cilantro chutney. Serve the kebabs with rice and/or grilled naan bread, plus yogurt or raita.

**TOMATO CHUTNEY**

2 lb (1 kg) plum tomatoes, halved lengthwise

3 tablespoons extra-virgin olive oil

Kosher salt and freshly ground pepper

½ yellow onion, minced

2 cloves garlic, minced

1 teaspoon yellow mustard seeds

½ teaspoon ground ginger

¼ teaspoon ground cinnamon

¼ cup (1¾ oz/50 g) sugar

3 tablespoons apple cider vinegar

**MAKES 6 SERVINGS**

To make the chutney, prepare a gas or charcoal grill for direct grilling over medium-high heat (400°–450°F/200°–230°C). Brush the grill grate clean. Scoop out and discard the seeds from the tomato halves, coat with 1 tablespoon of olive oil, and season with 2 tablespoons of salt and ¼ teaspoon of pepper. Put the tomatoes on the grate, cover the grill, and cook, turning once, until browned, about 4 minutes per side.

Transfer the tomatoes to a cutting board and let cool for a few minutes. Peel away the skin and discard. Chop the tomato flesh finely. Set aside.

In a saucepan over medium heat, warm the remaining 2 tablespoons of olive oil. Add the onion, garlic, mustard seeds, ginger, and cinnamon and cook, stirring, until the onion softens. Stir in the sugar, vinegar, and reserved tomatoes. Bring to a simmer and cook, stirring often, until the mixture thickens, about 15 minutes. Taste and adjust the seasoning with salt and pepper, if needed. Let cool completely. Transfer to an airtight container and refrigerate at least overnight or for up to 1 week.

*continued on page 96*

*continued from page 95*

**TANDOORI CHICKEN**

2 cups (1 lb/450 g) plain
whole-milk yogurt

2 tablespoons fresh
lemon juice

2 tablespoons minced peeled
fresh ginger

4 cloves garlic, minced

1 teaspoon *each*
ground coriander and
ground turmeric

½ teaspoon saffron threads

½ teaspoon ground cumin

½ teaspoon cayenne pepper,
or more as desired

Kosher salt and freshly
ground pepper

8 boneless, skinless chicken
thighs, cut into 1-inch
(2.5-cm) cubes

6 to 12 metal or
wooden skewers

1 small red onion, thinly
sliced and separated
into rings

¼ cup (½ oz/15 g) chopped
fresh cilantro

To make the tandoori chicken, in a bowl, whisk together the yogurt, lemon juice, ginger, garlic, coriander, turmeric, saffron, cumin, cayenne pepper, 1 teaspoon of salt, and ½ teaspoon of black pepper. Place the chicken cubes in a large resealable plastic bag and pour in the marinade. Seal the bag, squish the marinade around the chicken, and refrigerate overnight.

At least 30 minutes before you are ready to begin grilling, remove the chicken from the refrigerator. Discard the marinade. If using wooden skewers, soak them in water for 30 minutes.

Prepare a gas or charcoal grill for direct grilling over high heat (450°–550°F/230°–290°C). Brush the grill grate clean.

Thread the chicken cubes onto the skewers without crowding them. Place the skewers on the grill directly over the heat and cook, turning once, until the chicken is lightly grill-marked on both sides and opaque throughout but still moist, about 5 minutes on each side. If the chicken begins to burn, move the skewers to the edge of the grill or lower the heat of a gas grill.

Slide the chicken off the skewers onto a platter. Top with the onion and cilantro and serve at once with the tomato chutney alongside.

# Rotisserie Lemon-Tarragon Chicken

If your grill is set up with a rotisserie, this is a fast and easy way to get an exceptionally flavorful whole roasted chicken on the table with very little effort. Seasoning the chicken all over with salt then refrigerating it for up to 2 days dries out the skin and results in a super-crisp exterior when the chicken is roasted.

1 whole chicken, about
5 lb (2.3 kg), neck
and giblets removed

7 fresh tarragon sprigs, plus
2 tablespoons chopped leaves

Kosher salt and freshly
ground pepper

2 lemons, quartered

2 tablespoons extra-virgin
olive oil

½ cup (4 oz/115 g)
unsalted butter

**MAKES 6 SERVINGS**

Set a large wire rack on a rimmed baking sheet. Using your fingers, gently separate the chicken skin from the top of the breasts, thighs, and drumsticks, being careful not to tear the skin. Slide 1 tarragon sprig into each of the 6 pockets you have created. Season the chicken all over with 1 tablespoon of salt and ½ teaspoon of pepper, sprinkling a little inside the cavity, too. Place 4 of the lemon quarters and the remaining 1 tarragon sprig in the cavity. Using kitchen twine, tie the chicken legs together or truss the chicken so that it holds its shape. Place the chicken, breast side up, on the rack on the pan. (At this point, the chicken can be refrigerated, uncovered, for up to 2 days; the skin will dry and tighten over the meat.)

Remove the grate from the grill and set up a rotisserie in the grill. Prepare the grill for indirect medium heat (350°–450°F/180°–230°C). Secure the chicken on the spit, then rub the olive oil all over the chicken. Insert the spit into the rotisserie motor, making sure the chicken can rotate without touching the grill. Cover the grill and cook until the skin is golden and an instant-read thermometer inserted into the inside of a thigh away from bone registers 165°F (74°C), 1–1¼ hours.

Remove the spit from the rotisserie and place the chicken, still on the spit, on a cutting board. Let rest for 15 minutes.

Meanwhile, in a small saucepan over low heat, melt the butter and stir in the chopped tarragon.

Remove the chicken from the spit and tilt the bird to pour the juices from the cavity into the tarragon butter. Carve the chicken by removing the wings, cutting the legs into thighs and drumsticks, and removing each breast from the bone, then cutting each breast into 2 to 4 pieces. Pour the juices from the cutting board into the tarragon butter, transfer the tarragon butter to a serving bowl, and serve the tarragon butter and remaining lemon wedges alongside the chicken.

# Grilled Barbecue Chicken Pizza

If you love barbecued chicken, this is the pizza for you. Plus, this recipe is a terrific way to use up any leftover chicken you might have. Topped with smoky Cheddar cheese, thinly sliced red onion, sweet corn, and roasted peppers, along with a thick smear of your favorite barbecue sauce, it has everything you would ever want in a grilled pizza.

Extra-virgin olive oil

1 lb (450 g) pizza dough, homemade (page 174) or purchased

1 cup (8 fl oz/240 ml) Classic Barbecue Sauce (page 175), or your favorite barbecue sauce

2 cups chopped grilled chicken

2 cups (8 oz/225 g) grated smoked Cheddar cheese

1 small red onion, halved and sliced paper-thin

1 cup (6 oz/170 g) grilled corn kernels (page 49)

½ cup (2½ oz/70 g) chopped roasted red bell peppers

½ cup (1 oz/30 g) chopped fresh cilantro

Kosher salt

**MAKES 4 SERVINGS**

Prepare a gas or charcoal grill for direct grilling over medium heat on one side (350°–450°F/180°–230°C) and low heat on the other side (about 300°F/150°C). Brush the grill grate clean.

Brush four 12-inch (30-cm) squares of aluminum foil on one side with olive oil. Cut the dough into 4 equal pieces. Put a piece of dough in the center of a piece of foil and press and stretch the dough into a 10-inch (25-cm) round about ⅛ inch (3 mm) thick. Brush the top of the dough with olive oil. Repeat with the remaining pieces of dough and foil squares.

One at a time, invert each round of dough directly onto the hotter side of the grill. Using tongs and a spatula, peel the foil carefully off the dough. Grill until the dough is nicely browned on the bottom and almost dry on top, 1–2 minutes. After about 1 minute, use the tongs and the spatula to rotate the dough 90 degrees to prevent burning. Repeat with all the dough rounds.

Transfer the grilled dough rounds to a cutting board, with the grilled sides up. Spread ¼ cup of sauce over the grilled side of each round. Arrange the chicken, Cheddar, onion, corn, and bell peppers over the sauce, dividing the ingredients evenly among the pizzas. One at a time, lift the pizzas and place them back on the grill over the cooler side. Cover the grill and cook, rotating each round about 90 degrees halfway through the cooking, until the bottoms brown and the cheese melts, about 5 minutes.

Using a large spatula and tongs, transfer the pizzas to the cutting board. Top each with some of the cilantro and season with salt. Cut into wedges and serve.

# Shrimp Po'Boy Sliders with Rémoulade

Here, shrimp po'boys are transformed into mini burgers, making them a terrific addition to a New Orleans–inspired lunch or dinner. They are great for entertaining because the rémoulade and the patties can be made a day ahead, so all you have to do is fry the patties and serve. The rémoulade is also great alongside crab cakes.

RÉMOULADE

¾ cup (6 fl oz/180 ml) mayonnaise

2 tablespoons whole-grain mustard

2 tablespoons finely chopped shallot

2 tablespoons chopped fresh flat-leaf parsley

Kosher salt and freshly ground pepper

1 tablespoon fresh lemon juice and/or hot-pepper sauce

1 lb (450 g) medium shrimp, peeled, deveined, and diced

¼ cup (1¼ oz/35 g) minced yellow onion

¼ cup (1¼ oz/35 g) minced red bell pepper

3 tablespoons finely ground yellow cornmeal

2 tablespoons chopped fresh flat-leaf parsley

1 large egg, lightly beaten

½ teaspoon *each* garlic powder and onion powder

¼ teaspoon dried oregano

⅛ teaspoon cayenne pepper

Kosher salt and freshly ground pepper

2 teaspoons olive oil

14 slider buns, split

**MAKES 6 SERVINGS**

To make the rémoulade, in a bowl, stir together the mayonnaise, mustard, shallots, and parsley. Season with salt and pepper. Add lemon juice and/or hot-pepper sauce to taste, depending on how spicy you'd like the rémoulade to be. (The rémoulade will keep in the refrigerator in an airtight container for up to 1 week.)

In a bowl, combine the shrimp, onion, bell pepper, cornmeal, parsley, egg, garlic powder, onion powder, oregano, cayenne, and ¼ teaspoon each of salt and pepper. Using your hands, form the mixture into 14 patties and transfer to the refrigerator to chill for at least 30 minutes and up to overnight.

Warm the olive oil in a nonstick skillet over medium-high heat. Working in batches, add the patties and cook, turning once with a flat spatula, until cooked through, 3–4 minutes per side. Spread a dollop of rémoulade on the cut sides of the bun tops and bottoms. Set the patties on the buns. Close the sliders and serve right away.

# Grilled Shrimp with Romesco

Romesco is a Spanish sauce made from red peppers, almonds, and plenty of garlic and paprika. It is excellent on grilled meats and poultry, fish, and especially jumbo shrimp grilled alongside a bunch of green onions. Sweet piquillo peppers are sold in most well-stocked markets, but roasted red bell peppers can be substituted.

**ROMESCO**

1 jar (10½ oz/300 g) piquillo peppers, drained

½ cup (2½ oz/70 g) whole toasted almonds, chopped

¼ cup (2 fl oz/60 ml) extra-virgin olive oil

3 cloves garlic, chopped

2 teaspoons smoked paprika

Kosher salt and freshly ground pepper

12 jumbo shrimp, peeled and deveined

4 tablespoons (2 fl oz/60 ml) extra-virgin olive oil

4 cloves garlic, minced

2 teaspoons smoked paprika

16 green onions

2 lemons, halved crosswise

Kosher salt and freshly ground pepper

**MAKES 4 SERVINGS**

Prepare a gas or charcoal grill for direct grilling over medium heat (350°–450°F/180°–230°C). Brush the grill grate clean.

To make the romesco, in a blender, combine the piquillo peppers, almonds, olive oil, garlic, and paprika and process until smooth. Pour into a bowl and season with salt and pepper. Set aside at room temperature.

In a bowl, combine the shrimp, 2 tablespoons of olive oil, the garlic, and paprika and turn to coat the shrimp evenly. Coat the green onions and lemons lightly with the remaining 2 tablespoons of olive oil.

Arrange the shrimp on the grill directly over the heat and season with salt and pepper. Cook for about 3 minutes, then add the green onions and lemons, cut side down. Cook, turning all the items as needed, until the shrimp are opaque throughout and the green onions and lemons are lightly charred, about 6 minutes total for the shrimp and 3 minutes total for the green onions and lemons. Transfer the shrimp, green onions, and lemons to a platter and serve with the romesco sauce alongside.

# Whole Grilled Salmon with Cilantro Pesto

A whole salmon might seem like an extravagant, difficult thing to manage on the grill, but cutting slashes in the sides of the fish ensures that it cooks more evenly throughout while also staying moist. The homemade cilantro-almond pesto adds a bright and herbaceous element, but purchased basil pesto would be delicious as well.

**CILANTRO PESTO**

¼ cup (1 oz/30 g) slivered almonds, toasted

3 cups (6 oz/170 g) chopped fresh cilantro (about 2 bunches)

2 cloves garlic, chopped

¼ cup (2 fl oz/60 ml) extra-virgin olive oil

Kosher salt and freshly ground pepper

1 whole wild salmon, about 5 lb (2.3 kg), cleaned, with head, scales, and fins removed

2 lemons, halved

1 tablespoon extra-virgin olive oil

**MAKES 8 TO 10 SERVINGS**

Prepare a gas or charcoal grill for indirect grilling over medium heat (350°–450°F/ 180°–230°C). Brush the grill grate clean.

To make the pesto, in a food processor, pulse the almonds until chopped. Add the cilantro and garlic and process until all of the ingredients are finely chopped (or chop everything with a knife). Scrape into a bowl and mix in the olive oil, ½ teaspoon of salt, and ¼ teaspoon of pepper.

Moving from the tail to the head, scrape the dull side of a knife against the skin of the salmon to remove excess moisture and any fine scales. Cut 6 evenly spaced diagonal slashes through the flesh on each side of the fish down to the bone. Fill the slashes with the pesto and rub more pesto into the interior cavity. Any leftover pesto can be served with the salmon. Squeeze the juice from 1 lemon over the fish.

Coat the salmon on all sides with the olive oil. Place the salmon over indirect heat and cook, turning it over after about 10 minutes, until an instant-read thermometer inserted into the thickest part of the fish registers 130°F (54°C) or the fish barely flakes when gently pressed, about 20 minutes.

Transfer the fish to a platter. (If the skin tears while grilling, simply peel the skin off before serving.) Squeeze the juice from the remaining lemon over the fish. Use the slashes in the flesh to help portion the fish. Serve with any extra pesto.

# Smoked Salmon with Lemon-Garlic Aioli

The key to making hot-smoked salmon is to rub it first with a salt-and-sugar "cure" that helps draw out some of the moisture from the fillets and bring smoke into the meat. A short stint in the smoke-filled grill is all you need to create this dish. Serve it with the roasted garlic and lemon aioli alongside for dipping, or top a leafy green salad with chunks of the salmon and accompany it with thick slices of crusty bread alongside.

¼ cup (2 oz/60 g) firmly packed light brown sugar

¼ cup (2 oz/60 g) kosher salt

1 tablespoon chopped fresh dill

4 skin-on center-cut salmon fillets, each about ½ lb (225 g) and 1 inch (2.5 cm) thick, pin bones removed

**LEMON-GARLIC AIOLI**

2 cloves garlic, unpeeled

2 large egg yolks, fresh or pasteurized

Finely grated zest of 1 lemon

2 tablespoons fresh lemon juice, or more as desired

Kosher salt

½ cup (4 fl oz/120 ml) avocado or canola oil

About 2 cups applewood chips, soaked in water for 30 minutes

**MAKES 4 SERVINGS**

Set a large wire rack in a rimmed baking sheet. In a small bowl, stir together the sugar, salt, and dill. Lightly rub the mixture on all sides of the fillets, then place the fillets on the rack and cover the whole thing with plastic wrap. Refrigerate for 2 hours or up to 4 hours.

To make the aioli, preheat the oven to 350°F (180°C). Wrap the garlic in aluminum foil, place on a baking sheet, and bake until soft, about 40 minutes. (Alternatively, skip this step and substitute 1 tablespoon store-bought puréed roasted garlic.) Let the garlic cool, then squeeze the flesh into a mini food processor or a blender. Add the egg yolks and lemon zest and juice and pulse to combine. Sprinkle in a pinch of salt. With the machine running, slowly add the avocado oil in a thin, steady stream and process until the mixture thickens to the consistency of mayonnaise. Taste and adjust the seasoning, if needed. If the mixture seems too thick, thin it with a little warm water. Cover and refrigerate until ready to serve. (The aioli can be made up to 3 days in advance and refrigerated.)

Prepare a gas or charcoal grill for indirect grilling over medium heat (350°–450°F/ 180°–230°C). If using charcoal, bank the lit coals on either side of the grill bed, leaving a strip in the center without heat. Place a drip pan in the center strip and fill the pan with water. Add about 2 cups of wood chips to the fire just before grilling. If using gas, fill the smoker box with up to 2 cups of wood chips, then preheat the grill. Turn off 1 or more of the burners to create a cooler zone. Brush the grill grate clean.

Rinse the fish fillets under cold running water. Pat dry with paper towels. Place the fillets, skin side down, on the grill over the indirect heat area. Cover the grill and cook, without turning the fillets, until just opaque throughout, 15–20 minutes.

Transfer the salmon to a platter and serve warm or at room temperature with the aioli alongside.

# Coconut-Lime Halibut

Thick, grilled halibut fillets take a trip to the Caribbean with this tart-sweet coconut-lime sauce and plenty of roasted peanuts and fresh cilantro. Mayo might seem like a surprising choice to brush the fish with, but it acts as an excellent nonstick coating on the grill. Almost any thick white fish, like mahi-mahi, would work well, so purchase whatever is freshest in the market.

**COCONUT-LIME SAUCE**

1 jalapeño chile, seeded and minced

1 tablespoon avocado or canola oil

1 small red onion, minced

3 cloves garlic, minced

1 can (14 fl oz/425 ml) coconut milk

¼ cup (2 oz/60 g) cream of coconut

¼ cup (2 fl oz/60 ml) fresh lime juice

1 teaspoon honey

Kosher salt and freshly ground pepper

4 halibut fillets, each about ½ lb (225 g) and 1 inch (2.5 cm) thick

2 tablespoons mayonnaise

Kosher salt and freshly ground pepper

½ cup (2½ oz/70 g) dry-roasted peanuts, chopped

¼ cup (½ oz/15 g) chopped fresh cilantro

**MAKES 4 SERVINGS**

To make the sauce, in a saucepan over medium-high heat, cook the jalapeño, stirring occasionally, until it takes on a little color, about 2 minutes. Add the avocado oil, then add the onion and garlic and cook, stirring often, until softened, about 5 minutes. Add the coconut milk and cream of coconut, bring to a simmer, reduce the heat to maintain the simmer, and cook for 10 minutes to blend the flavors. Remove from the heat. Transfer the mixture to a blender and process until smooth, then return to the pan. Mix in the lime juice and honey and season with salt and pepper. Cover to keep warm.

Prepare a gas or charcoal grill for direct grilling over high heat (450°–550°F/230°–290°C). Brush the grill grate clean.

Brush the fish fillets on both sides with the mayonnaise, coating evenly. Season with salt and pepper. Place the fish on the grill directly over the heat and cook, turning once, until it is just opaque throughout and flakes when prodded gently with a fork, about 8 minutes total per inch of thickness.

Transfer the fillets to a platter. Ladle some of the warm coconut-lime sauce over each fillet, sprinkle with the peanuts and cilantro, and serve at once. Pass the remaining sauce at the table.

# Grilled Fish Tacos with Mexican Slaw

Lighter and healthier than their deep-fried counterparts, these grilled fish tacos are quick to pull together. Just make the slaw and salsa (or purchase them for an even faster preparation) ahead and grill the fillets and warm the tortillas when you are ready to eat. Any fresh, firm, and flaky white fish fillet will work well for these tacos.

1½ lb (680 g) red snapper, cod, or halibut fillets

Kosher salt and freshly ground pepper

Avocado or canola oil, for brushing

12 corn tortillas

Tomatillo-Avocado Salsa (page 110) or your favorite salsa

Mexican-Style Coleslaw (page 133)

¼ cup (2 oz/60 g) Mexican crema

½ cup (1 oz/30 g) chopped fresh cilantro

**MAKES 6 SERVINGS**

Prepare a gas or charcoal grill for direct grilling over medium-high heat (400°–450°F/200°–230°C). Brush the grill grate clean. Season the fish fillets with salt and pepper and brush lightly all over with avocado oil.

Place the fish directly over the heat. Cover the grill and cook, turning once, until the fish is opaque throughout and flakes when prodded with a fork, 6–10 minutes, depending on the thickness of the fillets. While the fish is cooking, warm the tortillas on the grill, then wrap them in aluminum foil to keep warm. Transfer the fish to a cutting board or baking sheet.

To assemble the tacos, fill each tortilla with some of the fish, then top with salsa and coleslaw. Drizzle with crema and garnish with the cilantro. Serve at once, passing any remaining salsa at the table.

# Crab Cake Burgers with Green Goddess & Watercress

This elegant recipe, combining burger-size crab cakes with green goddess dressing, fresh watercress, and tender brioche buns, would be perfect for a midsummer lunch party with your dearest friends. You can transform these into sliders by forming smaller patties and serving them on slider buns with torn butter lettuce and lemon-garlic aioli (page 104).

**GREEN GODDESS DRESSING**

1 ripe avocado, pitted and peeled

½ cup (4 oz/115 g) sour cream

1 clove garlic, chopped

1 green onion, chopped

2 tablespoons chopped fresh basil

1 tablespoon chopped fresh tarragon

1 tablespoon fresh lemon juice

1 tablespoon olive oil

Kosher salt and freshly ground pepper

**CRAB CAKE BURGERS**

1 lb (450 g) cooked fresh crabmeat, picked over for shells and cartilage

¼ cup (2 fl oz/60 ml) mayonnaise

¼ cup (1 oz/30 g) panko bread crumbs

¼ cup (½ oz/15 g) minced fresh cilantro

2 tablespoons finely chopped shallot

Kosher salt and freshly ground pepper

2 teaspoons olive oil

4 brioche buns, split and toasted

1 cup (1 oz/30 g) watercress

**MAKES 4 SERVINGS**

To make the dressing, in a food processor, combine all the ingredients and process until smooth, stopping to scrape down the sides of the bowl a few times. Season with salt and pepper. Transfer to a bowl.

To make the burgers, in a medium bowl, stir together the crabmeat, mayonnaise, bread crumbs, cilantro, and shallot. Season well with salt and pepper. Using your hands, form the mixture into 4 patties.

In a nonstick frying pan over medium-high heat, warm the olive oil. Add the crab patties and cook, turning once with a flat spatula, until cooked through, about 6 minutes per side.

Spread the cut sides of the buns generously with the green goddess. Set the crab burgers on the buns and top with the watercress, dividing it evenly among the burgers. Close the burgers and serve right away.

# Grilled Mahi-Mahi with Tomatillo-Avocado Salsa

The zesty tomatillo and avocado salsa used to top these grilled white fish fillets is endlessly versatile. This same dish can be easily be transformed into fish tacos by dividing chunks of the grilled fish between flour tortillas and topping each with big spoonfuls of the salsa. This dish would also be terrific with grilled corn and a simple mixed greens and avocado salad.

**TOMATILLO-AVOCADO SALSA**

5 oz (140 g) tomatillos (3 or 4), husked and rinsed

4 green onions, including about 6 inches (15 cm) of the green tops

1 tablespoon plus 1 teaspoon extra-virgin olive oil

½ small avocado, pitted, peeled, and diced

⅓ cup (⅔ oz/20 g) chopped fresh cilantro

½ jalapeño chile, seeded and minced

1 small clove garlic, minced

1 tablespoon fresh lime juice

1 teaspoon honey

Kosher salt

4 mahi-mahi fillets, each about 6 oz (170 g)

Extra-virgin olive oil, for brushing

Kosher salt and freshly ground pepper

**MAKES 4 SERVINGS**

Prepare a gas or charcoal grill for direct grilling over high heat (450°–550°F/230°–290°C). Brush the grill grate clean.

To make the salsa, brush the tomatillos and green onions with the 1 teaspoon of olive oil and place over the heat on the grill. Cook, turning once or twice, until lightly charred on both sides, 4–5 minutes for the onions and 6–8 minutes for the tomatillos. The tomatillos will have softened and started to release their juices.

Transfer the tomatillos to a food processor and the green onions to a cutting board. Coarsely chop the onions and add to the food processor along with the avocado, cilantro, jalapeño, garlic, the remaining 1 tablespoon of olive oil, the lime juice, honey, and ½ teaspoon of salt. Process until the mixture is smooth. Transfer to a bowl, then taste and adjust the seasoning with lime juice or salt, if needed.

Lightly brush the fish fillets on both sides with olive oil and then season on both sides with salt and pepper. Place the fillets on the grill over the heat. Cook, turning once about halfway through, until opaque throughout when tested with a knife tip, 8–10 minutes total.

Transfer the fillets to warmed individual plates. Spoon the salsa over the fish, dividing evenly, and serve.

# Fried Polenta with Creamy Chanterelle Mushrooms

The subtle quality of polenta makes it the perfect bed for the chanterelle mushrooms that top these crostini. Aficionados describe these trumpet-shaped mushrooms as having a fruity aroma akin to apricots. To avoid lumps, add the polenta to the water and stir constantly. Uncork a merlot or cabernet sauvignon to accompany these elegant crostini.

### FRIED POLENTA

1 bay leaf

Kosher salt and freshly ground pepper

2 tablespoons extra-virgin olive oil

1 cup (5½ oz/140 g) polenta

1 tablespoon unsalted butter

### CREAMY MUSHROOMS

¼ cup (2 oz/60 g) unsalted butter

3 shallots, minced

½ lb (225 g) chanterelle mushrooms, coarsely chopped

Kosher salt and freshly ground pepper

½ cup (4 oz/115 g) mascarpone cheese

2 tablespoons minced fresh flat-leaf parsley

Wedge of Parmesan cheese

### MAKES 8 SERVINGS

To make the fried polenta, in a saucepan over high heat, bring 4 cups (1 l) water to boil. Add the bay leaf, 1 tablespoon of salt, and 1 tablespoon of olive oil. Slowly add the polenta, stirring constantly. Reduce the heat to low and cook, stirring often, until the polenta pulls away from the sides of the pan, about 30 minutes. Remove and discard the bay leaf.

Rinse an 8-by-10-inch (20-by-25-cm) baking dish but do not dry it. Immediately pour the polenta into the dish. It should be about ½ inch (12 mm) thick. Set aside to cool until firm, about 30 minutes.

To make the mushrooms, in a large frying pan over medium heat, melt the butter. Add the shallots and cook until slightly wilted, about 2 minutes. Add the chanterelles, season with salt and pepper, and cook until golden brown and tender, about 4 minutes. Remove from the heat and set aside.

Cut the cooled polenta into pieces about 1 by 2 inches (2.5 by 5 cm). In another large frying pan, melt the butter with the remaining 1 tablespoon of olive oil over medium-high heat. Working in batches, fry the polenta pieces, turning once, until barely golden on both sides and heated through, about 3 minutes per side.

Arrange the polenta on a platter. Place a small dollop of mascarpone on each piece. Spoon the mushrooms over the mascarpone, dividing them evenly, and garnish with the parsley. Using a vegetable peeler or a cheese plane, shave a little Parmesan over each piece. Serve warm.

# Grilled Pizza with Fontina, Cherry Tomatoes, Olives & Arugula

Salty prosciutto drizzled with honey and hot-pepper sauce is a satisfying and unexpected combination for topping grilled pizzas. Make sure to grill one side of the pizza first to give it more structure. You can also use a grill-safe pizza stone to cook the pizzas, just heat it on the grill first before adding the topped pizza. A handful of arugula is a nice addition to these pizzas as well.

Extra-virgin olive oil, for brushing

1 lb (450 g) pizza dough, homemade (page 174) or purchased

3 cups (12 oz/340 g) shredded fontina, mozzarella, or other melting cheese

2 ripe but firm summer tomatoes, thinly sliced

1 small red onion, halved and thinly sliced

1 cup (5 oz/140 g) pitted Gaeta or Kalamata olives, halved

2 cups (2 oz/60 g) baby arugula

½ cup (1 oz/30 g) finely shredded fresh basil

Kosher salt

**MAKES 4 SERVINGS**

Prepare a gas or charcoal grill for direct grilling over medium heat on one side (350°–375°F/180°–190°C) and low heat on the other side (about 300°F/150°C). Brush the grill grate clean.

Brush four 12-inch (30-cm) squares of aluminum foil on one side with olive oil. Cut the dough into 4 equal pieces. Put a piece of dough in the center of a piece of foil and press and stretch the dough into a 10-inch (25-cm) round about ⅛ inch (3 mm) thick. Brush the top of the dough with olive oil. Repeat with the remaining dough and foil squares.

One at a time, invert each round of dough directly onto the hotter side of the grill, oiled side down. Using tongs and a spatula, peel the foil carefully off the dough. Grill until the dough is nicely browned on the bottom and almost dry on top, 1–2 minutes. After about 1 minute, use the tongs and the spatula to rotate the dough 90 degrees to prevent burning. Repeat with all the dough rounds.

Transfer the grilled dough rounds to a cutting board, with the grilled sides up. Top each round with ¾ cup (3 oz/90 g) of cheese and a few tomato slices. Scatter some of the onion and olives over the tomatoes. One at a time, lift the pizzas and place them back on the grill on the cooler side. Cover the grill and cook, rotating each pizza about 90 degrees halfway through the cooking, until the bottoms brown and the cheese melts, about 5 minutes.

Using a large spatula and tongs, transfer the pizzas to the cutting board. Top each with some of the arugula and basil. Drizzle with a little olive oil and sprinkle with salt. Cut into wedges and serve.

# Pasta with Eggplant, Tomatoes & Ricotta Salata

This Sicilian pasta dish, also known as pasta Norma, makes good use of the abundant eggplant found during the summer months most everywhere. Eggplant, with its meaty texture, is an excellent substitute for animal-based protein. The combination of ingredients may seem overly simple, but each one adds texture and nuance, resulting in a hearty vegetarian meal.

1 large or 2 medium Italian eggplants

Kosher salt and freshly ground pepper

¼ cup (2 fl oz/60 ml) extra-virgin olive oil, plus more for frying

1 yellow onion, minced

2 cloves garlic, minced

2–2½ lb (1–1.1 kg) fresh tomatoes, peeled, seeded, and chopped, or 1 can (28 oz/ 800 g) whole tomatoes, seeded and chopped, with juice

1 lb (450 g) dried spaghetti

½ cup (1 oz/30 g) chopped fresh basil

½ cup (2½ oz/70 g) coarsely grated ricotta salata cheese, plus more for garnish

½ cup (2 oz/60 g) freshly grated pecorino romano or Parmesan cheese

**MAKES 6 SERVINGS**

Trim the eggplant, then cut crosswise into slices ½ inch (12 mm) thick. Layer the slices in a colander set over a plate, sprinkling each layer with salt, and let stand for 30 minutes to drain. Rinse the eggplant slices quickly under cold running water and pat dry with paper towels.

Line a large platter or tray with paper towels and set it next to the stove. Pour the olive oil to a depth of ½ inch (12 mm) into a large, heavy frying pan and place over medium heat until hot. Working in batches, add the eggplant slices in a single layer, being careful not to crowd the pan. Fry, turning once, until lightly browned on both sides, about 8 minutes total. Using tongs, transfer the slices to the prepared platter to drain. Fry the remaining slices in the same way, adding more olive oil to the pan as needed. Drain the olive oil and wipe out the pan.

In the frying pan over medium heat, warm the ¼ cup (2 fl oz/60 ml) of olive oil. Add the onion and cook until tender, about 5 minutes. Add the garlic and cook until fragrant, about 30 seconds. Add the tomatoes and season with salt and pepper. Reduce the heat to low and simmer, uncovered, until the sauce has thickened, about 20 minutes.

Meanwhile, bring a large pot three-fourths full of water to a boil and add 2 tablespoons of salt. Add the spaghetti, stir well, and cook, stirring occasionally, until al dente, about 10 minutes or according to the package directions.

Just before the pasta is ready, remove the sauce from the heat. Chop the eggplant slices and stir into the tomato sauce along with the basil.

Drain the pasta and transfer it into a warmed serving bowl. Add the sauce, ricotta salata, and pecorino romano and stir and toss well to combine. Garnish with more ricotta salata and serve at once.

# Gemelli with Pesto, Potatoes & Green Beans

This classic Italian pasta dish pairs pasta with diced potatoes and green beans, all cooked in the same pot. Cooking the ingredients together saves saves time and imbues them with flavor. Be sure to save some of the pasta water to loosen the fragrant pesto sauce when tossing everything together. If you like, garnish the pasta with shards or shavings of fresh Parmesan or pecorino romano.

Kosher salt

1 lb (450 g) gemelli or fusilli pasta

1 large boiling potato, peeled and diced

¼ lb (115 g) green beans, trimmed and halved crosswise

1 cup (8 fl oz/240 ml) basil pesto, homemade (page 174) or purchased

**MAKES 4 TO 6 SERVINGS**

Bring a large pot of salted water to a boil over high heat. Add the pasta and potato and cook until the pasta is al dente and the potato is tender, 10–12 minutes. During the last 3 minutes of cooking, add the green beans.

Drain the pasta, potato, and beans, reserving about ½ cup (4 fl oz/120 ml) of the pasta water. Put the pasta, potato, and beans in a warmed large, shallow bowl. Add a large dollop of pesto to the bowl, then add a few tablespoons of the reserved pasta water to loosen the sauce. Toss well until evenly coated. The pesto should be creamy and coat the pasta well, with little excess. Add more pesto as needed and toss again. Serve at once.

# Grilled Vegetable Gyros with Cucumber-Mint Sauce

These vegetarian pocket sandwiches feature a medley of well-spiced grilled vegetables topped with a refreshing yogurt sauce. For a vegan version, choose a plant-based yogurt. The seasoned veggies are so good they can also be used to top a rice or grain bowl or be tossed with fresh pasta.

Kosher salt

2 teaspoons chili powder

1 teaspoon *each* ground cumin, garlic powder, dried oregano, and dried thyme

½ teaspoon ground cinnamon

1 zucchini, halved lengthwise and thinly sliced

1 red bell pepper, seeded and sliced

1 yellow pepper, seeded and sliced

1 red onion, halved and thinly sliced

½ lb (225 g) mushrooms, halved

2 tablespoons extra-virgin olive oil

### CUCUMBER-MINT SAUCE

2 cups (1 lb/450 g) plain Greek yogurt

1 cucumber, peeled, seeded, and chopped

2 cloves garlic, chopped

2 tablespoons chopped fresh mint

2 tablespoons fresh lemon juice

Kosher salt and freshly ground pepper

6 pita breads, halved and split open to form pockets

**MAKES 4 TO 6 SERVINGS**

In a large bowl, combine 2 teaspoons of salt, the chili powder, cumin, garlic powder, oregano, thyme, and cinnamon. Add the zucchini, bell peppers, onion, mushrooms, and olive oil and toss to combine. Set aside.

To make the sauce, in a food processor, combine the yogurt, cucumber, garlic, mint, and lemon juice and process until smooth. Season with salt and pepper and set aside.

Prepare a gas or charcoal grill for direct grilling over high heat (450°–550°F/230°–290°C). Brush the grill grate clean.

Place the vegetables in a grill basket or on a perforated grill pan and place on the grill. Cook, stirring occasionally, until the vegetables are fork-tender and browned all over, about 12 minutes.

Divide the vegetables among the pita pockets and drizzle with a generous helping of the sauce. Serve, passing the remaining sauce at the table.

# Poblano & Jack Quesadillas with Creamy Avocado Salsa

Even though these quesadillas only have three ingredients—tortillas, poblanos, and pepper jack cheese—the combination packs a punch. Cooked right on the grill, these quesadillas are a fun shared starter to any grilled Mexican-themed meal. The creamy salsa is terrific, but use your favorite purchased salsa if you'd like to save a bit of time in the kitchen.

**CREAMY AVOCADO SALSA**

½ cup (4 oz/115 g) sour cream

2 teaspoons whole-grain mustard

2 teaspoons fresh lime juice

1 avocado, pitted, peeled, and diced

Kosher salt and freshly ground pepper

4 poblano chiles

8 flour tortillas, 10 inches (25 cm) in diameter

½ lb (225 g) pepper jack cheese, grated

**MAKES 4 SERVINGS**

To make the salsa, in a bowl, whisk together the sour cream, mustard, and lime juice. Carefully fold in the avocado, then season with salt and pepper. Use right away, or cover and refrigerate for up to 2 days.

Prepare a gas or charcoal grill for direct grilling over medium-high heat (400°–450°F/200°–230°C). Brush the grill grate clean.

Place the poblano chiles on the grill directly over the heat and cook, turning as needed, until charred on all sides, 4–5 minutes. Transfer to a cutting board and let cool until they can be handled. Peel, stem, seed, and cut lengthwise into narrow strips.

Divide the tortillas evenly between 2 baking sheets. Divide the chile strips and cheese evenly among them, leaving a ½-inch (12-mm) border around the edge of each tortilla. Top each with a second tortilla.

Using a large, wide spatula, transfer each quesadilla to the grill directly over the heat. Cook for about 3 minutes, pressing on the top tortilla of each quesadilla with a spatula so that the tortillas will meld. Flip each quesadilla and cook until the cheese is melted and the tortillas are golden brown, 3–4 minutes. Transfer to a cutting board and cut each quesadilla into 6 wedges. Serve at once with the salsa.

# Lemon Risotto with Asparagus

A favorite pairing for springtime risotto, grassy asparagus and vibrant lemon are natural partners. The addition of cream adds a luxurious note to this classic dish. Don't be dissuaded by the amount of time needed to stir the risotto on the stovetop—just pour yourself a glass of the same dry white wine you are using in the risotto and enjoy!

Kosher salt and freshly ground pepper

1 lb (450 g) asparagus, woody ends removed

1 tablespoon unsalted butter

1 tablespoon extra-virgin olive oil

1 shallot, minced

3 fresh thyme sprigs

2 cups (14 oz/400 g) Arborio, Carnaroli, or other risotto rice

¼ cup (2 fl oz/60 ml) dry white wine

6 cups (48 fl oz/1.4 l) low-sodium chicken broth, warmed

2 teaspoons finely grated lemon zest

½ cup (4 fl oz/120 ml) heavy cream

½ cup (2 oz/60 g) freshly grated Parmesan cheese

2 tablespoons fresh lemon juice

2 tablespoons minced fresh flat-leaf parsley

**MAKES 6 SERVINGS**

Bring a saucepan two-thirds full of salted water to a boil over high heat. Add the asparagus and cook until crisp-tender, 2–3 minutes. Drain and rinse under cold water to stop the cooking. Cut into 1-inch (2.5-cm) pieces and set aside.

In a large saucepan over medium heat, melt the butter with the olive oil. When the butter has melted, add the shallot and cook, stirring often, until starting to soften, about 5 minutes. Stir in the thyme sprigs and cook until the shallot is softened and translucent, about 3 minutes longer.

Add the rice and 1 teaspoon of salt, stirring to coat the grains with the butter and olive oil. Raise the heat to medium-high, pour in the wine, and stir until absorbed. Reduce the heat to medium and add a ladleful of the warm broth.

Cook, stirring often, until the broth is absorbed. Reduce the heat to medium-low, if necessary, to maintain a gentle simmer. Continue to cook the risotto, adding the broth one ladleful at a time and stirring until it is absorbed, until the rice is tender but still pleasantly chewy, about 20 minutes.

Stir in the reserved asparagus, lemon zest, cream, and Parmesan. Then stir in the lemon juice and a final ladleful of broth to achieve a creamy texture. The risotto should not be too stiff or too runny; it should mound softly on a spoon. Sprinkle with the parsley, season with pepper, and serve.

# Black Bean Burgers with Sriracha Mayo & Sesame Slaw

There are many tricks for making vegetable burgers taste meaty. You can add mushrooms to up the umami; season with cumin and smoked salt to lead the taste buds toward chili con carne and grilled meat; stir in some beans for a creamy mouthfeel reminiscent of well-marbled steak; and throw in a shredded beet for some rare-meat redness. These burgers have it all.

**BLACK BEAN BURGERS**

2 teaspoons extra-virgin olive oil, plus more for brushing

¾ cup (3¾ oz/105 g) finely chopped red onion

1 cup (3 oz/90 g) finely chopped cremini or button mushrooms

1 teaspoon ground cumin

1 teaspoon smoked paprika

Kosher salt and freshly ground pepper

1 can (15 oz/425 g) black beans, rinsed and drained

¾ cup (4½ oz/130 g) cooked quinoa

1 cup (2 oz/50 g) shredded raw beet

1 tablespoon soy sauce, preferably shoyu

½ cup (2 oz/60 g) ground walnuts

1 tablespoon canola oil

6 buns, split

Sriracha Mayo (page 177)
Sesame Slaw (page 134)

**MAKES 6 SERVINGS**

To make the black bean burgers, in a large frying pan over medium heat, warm the olive oil. Add the onion and mushrooms and cook until tender, about 4 minutes. Remove from the heat and season with the cumin, paprika, 1 teaspoon of salt, and ½ teaspoon of pepper. Add the beans and mash with the back of a fork into a chunky purée. There should be no whole beans but some visible chunks. Stir in the quinoa, beet, soy sauce, and walnuts. Using your hands, form the mixture into 6 patties. Coat the patties on both sides with the oil and set aside on a plate or baking sheet.

Prepare a gas or charcoal grill for direct grilling over medium heat (350°–450°F/180°–230°C). Brush the grill grate clean. Put a grill screen on the grill and oil the screen. Heat the screen for at least 5 minutes. Put the patties on the hot screen, cover the grill (with the vents completely open), and grill the burgers, turning once, until browned and heated through, about 5 minutes per side. To toast the buns, place them, cut side down, directly over the heat 1 minute before the burgers are ready. (Alternatively, cook the burgers in a hot cast-iron pan over medium heat and toast the buns under the broiler.)

To assemble the burgers, spread sriracha mayo on the grilled sides of each bun. Top the bottom buns with burger patties, then place a generous dollop of slaw on the patty. Place the bun top on the slaw, slightly askew to one side. You will probably have more slaw than can fit on the burgers; serve the remainder on the side.

# Falafel Burgers with Tahini-Cilantro Sauce

Falafel is a mainstay of Middle Eastern vegetarian meals, and they are never better than when you make them at home. These delicate burgers are best seared on the stovetop rather than grilled. Transform this into a hearty salad bowl by omitting the pita and serving the patties on a bed of romaine lettuce and chopped tomatoes, drizzled with the tahini-cilantro sauce.

**TAHINI-CILANTRO SAUCE**

¾ cup (6 oz/170 g) plain whole-milk yogurt

2 tablespoons tahini

2 tablespoons chopped fresh cilantro

2 teaspoons fresh lemon juice

½ teaspoon ground cumin

Kosher salt

**FALAFEL BURGERS**

1 can (15 oz/425 g) chickpeas, rinsed and drained

¼ cup (1¼ oz/35 g) finely diced red onion

¼ cup (¼ oz/7 g) lightly packed fresh flat-leaf parsley leaves

3 tablespoons fine dried bread crumbs

2 cloves garlic

1 large egg

1 teaspoon ground cumin

1 teaspoon ground coriander

Kosher salt

2 teaspoons extra-virgin olive oil

2 large pita breads, halved

1 cup (1¾ oz/50 g) shredded romaine lettuce

2 ripe plum tomatoes, chopped

**MAKES 4 SERVINGS**

To make the sauce, whisk together the yogurt, tahini, cilantro, lemon juice, cumin, and ½ teaspoon of salt until thoroughly combined. Set aside at room temperature until ready to serve or make up to 3 days in advance and store in the refrigerator in an airtight container.

To make the falafel burgers, in a food processor or blender, combine the chickpeas, onion, parsley, bread crumbs, garlic, egg, cumin, coriander, and 1 teaspoon of salt. Pulse until the mixture is mostly smooth, stopping to scrape down the sides of the bowl as needed. Using your hands, form the mixture into 8 small patties. Set aside.

In a nonstick frying pan over medium-high heat, warm the olive oil. Add the falafel burgers and cook, turning once, until golden brown and cooked through, about 3 minutes per side.

Place 2 falafel burgers in each pita half and fill with the lettuce, tomatoes, and a generous helping of the sauce. Serve right away.

sides

# Oaxacan Grilled Corn on the Cob

In Mexico, elotes—grilled ears of corn slathered with crema, crumbled cheese, chile powder, cilantro, and lime—are a common sight with street vendors. These are best in the summer, when corn is at its sweetest. Grill the corn in the husk, which helps steam it to perfection, then peel back the husks and use them as a handle.

½ cup (4 oz/115 g)
Mexican crema, sour cream,
or crème fraîche

¼ cup (2 fl oz/60 ml)
mayonnaise

⅓ cup (1½ oz/40 g) plus
3 tablespoons finely
crumbled Cotija or grated
pecorino romano cheese

1 tablespoon ancho
chile powder, plus more
for garnish

Kosher salt

4 ears corn in the husk

1 tablespoon minced
fresh cilantro

4 lime wedges, for serving

**MAKES 4 SERVINGS**

Prepare a gas or charcoal grill for direct grilling over medium-high heat (400°–450°F/200°–230°C). Brush the grill grate clean.

In a small bowl, combine the crema, mayonnaise, ⅓ cup (1½ oz/40 g) of cheese, the chile powder, and ½ teaspoon of salt and mix well.

Put the corn directly over the heat and cook, turning a few times, until the husks are charred all over, 10–13 minutes. Using heatproof grilling gloves, pull back the husks to expose the corn kernels, and pull off and discard the silks. Return the corn to the grill and continue to cook until the kernels are lightly browned all over, 5–8 minutes. Transfer the ears to a platter. Tie back the husks with a piece of the husk or kitchen string.

Brush the corn kernels all over with the crema mixture and then sprinkle with the remaining 3 tablespoons of cheese, a little ancho powder, and the cilantro. Serve with the lime wedges for squeezing.

# Grilled Ratatouille

With its base of eggplant, peppers, tomatoes, and zucchini, there are few dishes that make use of summer vegetables more than ratatouille. From the French word *ratouiller,* meaning "to stir up," this dish is served as a thick, coarse vegetarian stew, as either a main dish—try it over pasta or with a side of crusty bread—or as a side dish with grilled fish.

2 small Italian eggplants, about 1 lb (450 g) total

Kosher salt

1 large red bell pepper

1 large green bell pepper

1 large yellow onion, thickly sliced

2 ripe but firm tomatoes, halved crosswise

¼ cup (2 fl oz/60 ml) extra-virgin olive oil

2 zucchini or yellow summer squashes, cut lengthwise into slices ¼ inch (6 mm) thick

1 clove garlic, minced

½ teaspoon *each* chopped fresh thyme and red pepper flakes

1 tablespoon chopped fresh dill

**MAKES 4 TO 6 SERVINGS**

Trim the eggplant, then cut lengthwise into slices ¼ inch (6 mm) thick. Layer the slices in a colander set over a plate, sprinkling each layer with salt, and let stand, turning once, for 30 minutes to drain. Rinse the eggplant slices quickly under cold running water and pat dry with paper towels.

Prepare a gas or charcoal grill for direct grilling over high heat (450°–550°F/230°–290°C). Brush the grill grate clean.

Brush the eggplant slices, bell peppers, onion slices, and tomato halves with about 2 teaspoons of the olive oil. Place the eggplant around the edges of the grill and the peppers, onions, and tomato halves in the center. Cover the grill and open the vents. Cook, turning occasionally, until the eggplant and tomatoes are just tender and the bell peppers and onions are tender and well charred on all sides, about 10 minutes for the tomatoes, 15 minutes for the eggplant, and 25 minutes for the peppers and onions. As the vegetables are ready, transfer them to a cutting board. Tent the peppers with aluminum foil and let stand for about 10 minutes. As the other vegetables are removed from the rack, place the zucchini slices on the grill. Cook, turning once, until tender, about 5 minutes on each side.

Peel, stem, and seed the peppers, then cut them into short strips. Coarsely chop the tomatoes and zucchini. Cut the eggplant crosswise into narrow strips. Chop the onion. Add all of the vegetables to a serving bowl. Add the remaining 3 tablespoons of olive oil, the garlic, thyme, and red pepper flakes. Toss lightly to mix. Season with salt and toss again.

Sprinkle with the chopped dill and serve warm or at room temperature.

# Grill-Roasted Sesame Brussels Sprouts

This might seem like a surprising method for cooking brussels sprouts, but the grill adds smoky nuance to the tiny, slightly bitter cabbages. This version amps up the flavor with slightly spicy Korean ssamjang sauce and toasted sesame oil. The sprouts would be great served with grilled pork or beef and steamed rice.

16 brussels sprouts, stem end trimmed and halved lengthwise

2 tablespoons toasted sesame oil

Extra-virgin olive oil, for brushing

½ cup (5½ oz/160 ml) ssamjang sauce, homemade (page 76) or purchased

2 teaspoons sesame seeds, toasted

**MAKES 4 SERVINGS**

Prepare a gas or charcoal grill for direct and indirect grilling over medium heat (350°–450°F/180°–230°C). Brush the grill grate clean. Put a grill screen or perforated grill pan on the grill directly over the heat.

In a bowl, toss the brussels sprouts with the sesame oil, coating them evenly. Oil the grill screen. Put the sprouts, cut side down, on the hot screen and cook until browned, about 3 minutes.

Using tongs, move the screen away from the heat, then turn the sprouts browned side up. Brush with the ssamjang, cover the grill, and roast the sprouts until fork-tender, about 15 minutes.

Transfer the sprouts to a serving dish, sprinkle with the sesame seeds and serve right away.

# Zucchini with Capers,
## s & Orange Vinaigrette

t in the summer months, can sometimes be bland, but here it is
ooked over a hot fire then doused with an intense vinaigrette, toasted
salty-zesty capers. The vinaigrette uses a base of orange marmalade, doing
double duty for sweetness and zing. Serve this as part of a vegetarian meal with other grilled
vegetables and potatoes, or alongside grilled fish fillets.

**ORANGE VINAIGRETTE**

¼ cup (2½ oz/70 g)
orange marmalade

3 tablespoons red
wine vinegar

1 teaspoon Dijon mustard

½ clove garlic, minced

Kosher salt and freshly
ground pepper

¼ cup (2 fl oz/60 ml)
extra-virgin olive oil

1 tablespoon chopped
fresh basil

2 zucchini, about ¾ lb
(340 g) total

1 tablespoon extra-virgin
olive oil

Kosher salt and freshly
ground pepper

1 tablespoon small capers

1 tablespoon pine nuts,
preferably toasted

**MAKES 4 SERVINGS**

To make the vinaigrette, in a small bowl, whisk together the marmalade, vinegar, mustard, garlic, ⅛ teaspoon of salt, and ⅛ teaspoon of pepper. Add the olive oil in a thin, steady stream while whisking constantly until emulsified. Whisk in the basil. (The dressing can be refrigerated in an airtight container for up to 1 week.)

Prepare a gas or charcoal grill for direct grilling over medium heat (350°–450°F/ 180°–230°C). Brush the grill grate clean.

Trim the ends from the zucchini and then slice lengthwise into slices about ½ inch (12 mm) thick. Coat the slices all over with the olive oil, 1 teaspoon of salt, and ½ teaspoon of pepper. Put the zucchini on the grate and cook, turning once, until grilled marked, 2–3 minutes per side.

Transfer to a platter and scatter the capers and pine nuts over the top. Drizzle with some of the vinaigrette and serve. Pass additional vinaigrette alongside.

# Kitchen Sink Corn Bread

This corn bread has a little something for everyone: sweet corn kernels, sharp Cheddar cheese, and mild green chiles and red bell pepper. The buttermilk batter is lightly sweetened with honey and a snap to whisk together. Serve it directly from the cast-iron pan for a fun presentation, along with plenty of salted butter. If you like, you can omit the cheese, chiles, roasted peppers, and corn kernels for a simplified version.

1 cup (5 oz/140 g)
fine cornmeal

1 cup (4 oz/115 g)
all-purpose flour

2 teaspoons baking powder

½ teaspoon baking soda

Kosher salt

1 cup (6 oz/170 g) corn
kernels, preferably fresh

2 large eggs

¼ cup (3 oz/90 g) honey

1⅓ cups (11 fl oz/325 ml)
buttermilk

¼ cup (2 oz/60 g) unsalted
butter, melted, plus more
for serving

½ cup (2 oz/60 g) grated
sharp white Cheddar cheese

1 can (4 oz/115 g)
chopped green chiles,
drained and rinsed

¼ cup (1½ oz/40 g)
minced roasted
red bell pepper

**MAKES ONE 10-INCH
(25-CM) CORN BREAD**

Preheat the oven to 425°F (220°C). Generously butter a 10-inch (25-cm) cast-iron frying pan or a 9-inch (23-cm) square baking pan.

In a bowl, whisk together the cornmeal, flour, baking powder, baking soda, and ½ teaspoon of salt. Stir in the corn kernels.

In a large bowl, whisk together the eggs until blended. Add the honey, buttermilk, and melted butter and whisk until blended. Add the cornmeal mixture and stir until evenly moistened. Add the cheese, chiles, and roasted pepper and stir until just combined.

Scrape the batter into the prepared pan and smooth the top. Bake until a toothpick inserted into the center comes out clean, 20–25 minutes. Transfer the pan to a wire rack to cool slightly. Serve warm with lots of butter.

# Creamy Coleslaw

A classic at any backyard barbecue, creamy coleslaw is a cooling side dish and perfect alongside smoked ribs slathered in spicy barbecue sauce. The slaw couldn't be easier when prepared with the slicing and shredding blades of a food processor; however, you can also slice the cabbage with a chef's knife and shred the apple, onion, and carrots on the large holes of a box grater-shredder.

1 small head green cabbage

2 ribs celery

1 Granny Smith apple

½ small yellow or red onion

2 small carrots, peeled

2 tablespoons apple cider vinegar

1¼ cups (10 fl oz/300 ml) mayonnaise

2 tablespoons minced fresh flat-leaf parsley

Kosher salt and freshly ground pepper

Sugar (optional)

**MAKES 6 TO 8 SERVINGS**

Cut the cabbage into wedges through the stem end, then cut out the core from each wedge. Using a food processor fitted with the slicing blade, slice the cabbage into thin slivers. Transfer to a large bowl. Then slice the celery the same way and add it to the cabbage.

Replace the slicing blade with the shredding blade. Halve and core the apple but do not peel. Cut the apple and the onion into wedges. Shred the apple, onion, and carrots. Add to the cabbage and celery.

Sprinkle the vegetables with the vinegar and toss to coat evenly. Add the mayonnaise and parsley. Mix well. Season with salt and pepper. If you prefer a sweeter coleslaw, stir in a little sugar until the flavor suits you.

Cover and refrigerate until chilled, at least 2 hours. Taste and adjust the seasoning, if needed, with more vinegar, salt, and pepper before serving. Serve chilled.

# Mexican-Style Coleslaw

This endlessly versatile coleslaw is a snap to make and a terrific side [to a]
Mexican-inspired meal. Using green and red cabbage, along with ora[nge(s?)]
a colorful dish, but you can opt for one type of cabbage or another. [Add]
of chopped fresh cilantro to the slaw. Serve this atop fish tacos (page [__)]
skirt steak (page 72).

2 tablespoons extra-virgin olive oil

Finely grated zest and juice of 1 lime

1 teaspoon honey

1 clove garlic, minced

1 small jalapeño chile, seeded and minced

Kosher salt and freshly ground pepper

1 heaping cup (3 oz/90 g) shredded green cabbage

1 heaping cup (3 oz/90 g) shredded red cabbage

1 large carrot, shredded (about ¾ cup)

**MAKES 4 SERVINGS**

In a large bowl, stir together the olive oil, lime zest and juice, honey, garlic, and jalapeño. Season well with salt and pepper.

Stir in the green cabbage, red cabbage, and carrot and toss until well coated with the dressing. Let the slaw stand at room temperature for about 10 minutes, stir again, and serve right away.

# ...ame Slaw

...runchy, creamy slaw is the long-time sidekick to a sunny barbecue, and fresh cabbage is the key to a perfect slaw. Opt for a cabbage that feels weighty in hand with firm, unblemished leaves. A sharp chef's knife or a mandoline is preferred for shredding, as dull tools and food processors can wilt the leaves.

1 lb (450 g) napa cabbage (about ½ head), finely sliced

Kosher salt

¼ cup (2 fl oz/60 ml) Sriracha Mayo (page 177)

2 tablespoons soy sauce, such as Japanese white soy sauce

1 tablespoon rice vinegar

½ teaspoon honey

4 teaspoons toasted sesame oil

4 red radishes, halved lengthwise and thinly sliced crosswise

½ avocado, pitted, peeled, and diced

3 tablespoons toasted sesame seeds

**MAKES 4 SERVINGS**

In a large bowl, mix together the cabbage and 1 teaspoon of salt. Let stand for 20 minutes. During that time, the cabbage will soften and leach out much of its water. Using your hands, pick up the cabbage and put it on a clean flat-weave kitchen towel. Wrap the towel around the cabbage, hold it over a sink, and squeeze hard to rid the cabbage of most of its water. Rinse out the bowl and return the cabbage to it. Add the mayo, soy sauce, vinegar, honey, sesame oil, radishes, avocado, and sesame seeds and toss to combine evenly. Cover and refrigerate until needed.

# Drunken Pinto Beans

Simmering these slow-cooked beans in a dark beer adds richness to this popular side dish. A hint of smokiness comes from plenty of bacon, and the vegetables add subtle aroma. They are cut into large pieces and removed at the ends. Be sure to soak the beans overnight for a more tender result.

3 ribs celery

2 carrots

1 yellow onion

4 fresh thyme sprigs

1 lb (450 g) dried pinto beans, soaked in cold water overnight

6 slices thick-cut applewood smoked bacon, chopped

4 cloves garlic

1 bottle (12 fl oz/350 ml) dark beer, such as a porter or stout

Kosher salt and freshly ground pepper

**MAKES 10 SERVINGS**

Cut the celery, carrots, and onion into large chunks. Tie the thyme sprigs together with kitchen twine. Drain the beans and place in a slow cooker or a large, heavy pot over the stovetop. Add the bacon, garlic, celery, carrots, onion, beer, and thyme and stir to mix. Add water to cover the beans by about 1 inch (2.5 cm). If using a slow cooker, cover and cook on the low setting for about 10 hours or on the high setting for about 6 hours, until the beans are tender. If using a pot, bring the mixture to a boil over high heat, then reduce the heat to low and cook until tender, about 3 hours.

Remove and discard the onion, celery, and carrot chunks and the thyme sprigs. Season the beans with salt and pepper. Serve at once. Or, let cool, cover, and refrigerate for 1 day for the best flavor, then reheat gently to serve.

# Grilled Baby Artichokes with Spicy Garlic Butter

Artichokes have a subtle taste ideal for pairing with garlicky, lemon-kissed butter. While artichokes are often steamed or baked, grilling them makes them a natural partner to an alfresco meal. Be sure to choose larger baby artichokes, not the very small ones.

4 wooden skewers, soaked in water for 30 minutes

¼ cup (2 oz/60 g) unsalted butter

3 cloves garlic, minced

2 tablespoons fresh lemon juice

⅛ teaspoon red pepper flakes, or more as desired

Hot-pepper sauce

Kosher salt and freshly ground pepper

8 fresh baby artichokes, about 1 lb (450 g) total

**MAKES 4 SERVINGS**

Prepare a gas or charcoal grill for direct grilling over medium heat (350°–450°F/ 180°–230°C). Brush the grill grate clean.

In a small saucepan over medium-low heat, melt the butter. Add the garlic, lemon juice, red pepper flakes, and 1 or 2 dashes of hot-pepper sauce and stir to mix. Season to taste with salt and pepper. Remove from the heat and cover to keep warm.

Bang each artichoke on a countertop a couple of times. This will loosen the outer leaves and let the butter mixture penetrate better. Cut the artichokes in half lengthwise, trim the stems, and using a small spoon, scoop out the hairy choke. Slide the artichoke halves onto the skewers with the cut sides all facing the same way.

Place the artichokes, cut side down, on the grill directly over the heat and cook for about 5 minutes. Brush with the butter mixture and cook for another 5 minutes. Turn the artichokes, brush the cut side with the butter mixture, and continue cooking, turning and brushing with the butter mixture about every 5 minutes, for 20–25 minutes longer, taking care not to burn them. The artichokes are done if they give easily when you press into the middle of the cut side.

Transfer the artichokes to a platter and pour any remaining butter mixture over them. To eat the artichokes, peel off and discard the tough first layer or two of leaves, and eat the tender inner leaves.

# Classic Potato Salad

Nothing says picnic or backyard gathering quite like a big bowl of classic potato salad. This savory version is updated with whole-grain mustard, green onions, and fresh herbs. For an old-school rendition, swap out the green onions for ¼ cup (1½ oz/40 g) minced red or white onion, use yellow mustard instead of whole-grain, and add ¼ cup (1¼ oz/35 g) *each* finely chopped bread-and-butter pickles and hard-boiled eggs. For a crowd, you can double the recipe.

3 lb (1.4 kg) small yellow potatoes, halved if large

Kosher salt and freshly ground pepper

3 tablespoons white wine vinegar

1 cup (8 fl oz/240 ml) mayonnaise

2 tablespoons whole-grain mustard

4 ribs celery, finely diced

4 green onions, including tender green parts, chopped

2 tablespoons minced fresh flat-leaf parsley

**MAKES 8 SERVINGS**

In a large saucepan over high heat, combine the potatoes with salted water to cover, cover the pan, and bring to a boil. Uncover, reduce the heat to medium-low, and simmer until the potatoes are tender when pierced with a knife, about 25 minutes.

Drain the potatoes, then rinse them under cold running water until they are cool enough to handle. Cut the potatoes into ½-inch (12-mm) chunks and place in a large bowl. Sprinkle with the vinegar. Let cool completely.

In a small bowl, stir together the mayonnaise and mustard. Add to the cooled potatoes along with the celery, green onions, and parsley and mix gently. Season with salt and pepper.

Cover and refrigerate until chilled, at least 2 hours. Serve chilled.

# Cheesy Olive Pull-Apart Bread

Transform a simple loaf of crusty bread into a cheesy, olive-packed masterpiece. All you really need is a sharp bread knife and a hot oven. Nutty Gruyère cheese paired with briny Kalamata olives makes for a bright, tangy duo, but other combinations would also be terrific, such as fontina and green olives, crumbled gorgonzola and crisp bacon, or Cheddar and sliced green onions. A dipping plate filled with a grassy, zingy olive oil is a simple accompaniment that easily elevates this go-to side.

1 round loaf crusty bread, such as levain or sourdough

1½ cups (6 oz/170 g) shredded Gruyère cheese

½ cup (2½ oz/70 g) Kalamata olives, pitted and coarsely chopped

⅓ cup (⅓ oz/10 g) fresh flat-leaf parsley leaves, chopped

¼ cup (2 oz/60 g) unsalted butter, melted

**MAKES 4 TO 6 SERVINGS**

Preheat the oven to 350°F (180°C).

Using a long serrated knife, make cuts in the bread about 1 inch (2.5 cm) apart, being careful to not cut all the way through and leaving about ½ inch (12 mm) on the bottom. Rotate the bread so that you can make 1-inch (2.5-cm) cuts in the opposite direction.

In a bowl, stir together the cheese, olives, and parsley. Using your hands, stuff the cheese mixture between the cuts, working in both directions. Place the loaf on a baking sheet and drizzle the butter all over the top. Cover with aluminum foil and bake for 15 minutes. Remove the foil and continue to bake until the cheese is melted and the top of the bread is golden brown, about 10 minutes longer. Transfer to a plate and serve.

# Red Potato & Green Bean Salad with Herb Vinaigrette

Boldly flavored with olives, capers, and fresh mint, this bright and hearty salad is an updated riff on traditional three-bean salad, with small red potatoes added for heft. It would easily be at home as a satisfying vegetarian lunch or as a hearty side dish to grill-roasted chicken.

Kosher salt and freshly ground pepper

¼ lb (115 g) fresh green beans, trimmed

1¼ red potatoes, quartered

1 tablespoon whole-grain mustard

1 tablespoon red wine vinegar

1 tablespoon extra-virgin olive oil

1 cup (5 oz/140 g) canned chickpeas, drained and rinsed

½ small red onion, minced

½ cup (1 oz/30 g) coarsely chopped fresh flat-leaf parsley

½ cup (1 oz/30 g) coarsely chopped fresh mint

4 Sicilian or other green olives, pitted and coarsely chopped

1 tablespoon capers, rinsed and chopped

**MAKES 4 SERVINGS**

Prepare a large bowl of ice water. Bring a large pot of water to a boil over high heat, add 1 tablespoon of salt and the green beans, and cook until bright green and crisp-tender, about 3 minutes. Using a slotted spoon, transfer the beans to the bowl of ice water and let stand for 1–2 minutes. (Leave the pot on the heat.) Drain the beans and place in a large bowl. Add the potatoes to the boiling water and cook until just tender, about 10 minutes. Drain and let cool.

In a small bowl, whisk together the mustard, vinegar, 1 teaspoon of salt, and ⅛ teaspoon of pepper. Gradually whisk in the olive oil until blended.

Add the chickpeas, onion, parsley, mint, olives, capers, and the cooled potatoes to the bowl with the green beans. Pour the dressing over the salad and toss to coat. Let the salad stand for about 15 minutes to blend the flavors, then serve.

# Sweet Potato Fries
# with Homemade Ranch

Leaving the peels on sweet potato oven fries makes them both easier to prepare and healthier for you. Be sure to spread the wedges out so they aren't touching for the crispiest result. The homemade ranch is optional, but definitely worth the extra effort.

**HOMEMADE RANCH**

½ cup (4 fl oz/120 ml) mayonnaise

½ cup (4 fl oz/120 ml) buttermilk

1 tablespoon minced fresh flat-leaf parsley or 1 teaspoon dried parsley

1 teaspoon minced shallot or ½ teaspoon onion powder

1 clove garlic, minced, or ½ teaspoon garlic powder

Kosher salt and freshly ground pepper

Chopped fresh dill, for garnish (optional)

2½ lb (1.1 kg) sweet potatoes, scrubbed well

2 tablespoons extra-virgin olive oil

Kosher salt and freshly ground pepper

**MAKES 6 SERVINGS**

To make the ranch, in a bowl, combine the mayonnaise, buttermilk, parsley, shallot, garlic, ½ teaspoon of salt, and ¼ teaspoon of pepper. Stir until blended, then taste and adjust the seasoning, if needed. Transfer to a serving bowl and set aside until ready to serve, or cover and refrigerate for up to 3 days. Sprinkle with fresh dill, if using, just before serving.

Place a rack in the upper third of the oven and preheat to 450°F (230°C). Trim the ends from the sweet potatoes. Cut lengthwise into ½-inch-thick (12-mm-thick) slices, then cut each slice lengthwise into ½-inch-thick (12-mm-thick) sticks. Place the sticks in a large bowl, drizzle with the olive oil, and toss to coat evenly. Season well with salt and pepper. Place the sticks in a single layer on a large baking sheet, allowing ample space on all sides to ensure even cooking. Bake, turning once halfway, until golden and tender when pierced with a knife, about 30 minutes.

Serve hot with the ranch alongside for dipping.

# desserts

# Roasted Strawberry Shortcakes

Similar to biscuits or British-style scones, shortcakes are a popular American dessert. The key to tender, flaky shortcakes is to avoid overworking the dough. Cutting the dough into squares means you can use all of the dough in the first cutting rather than patting scraps back together. Most versions of shortcakes use raw strawberries, but roasting the berries make them intensely rich and sweet.

**ROASTED STRAWBERRIES**

1½ lb (680 g) strawberries, hulled and halved or quartered if large

⅓ cup (2½ oz/70 g) sugar

2 teaspoons fresh lemon juice

⅛ teaspoon vanilla extract

Kosher salt

**SHORTCAKES**

2 cups (9 oz/250 g) all-purpose flour, plus more for dusting

1 tablespoon baking powder

Kosher salt

2 tablespoons sugar, plus more for sprinkling

1 teaspoon finely grated lemon zest

6 tablespoons (3 oz/90 g) cold unsalted butter, cut into small pieces

1 cup (8 fl oz/240 ml) heavy cream, plus more for brushing

Whipped Cream (page 177)

**MAKES 6 SERVINGS**

To make the roasted strawberries, preheat the oven to 375°F (190°C). Line a rimmed baking sheet with parchment paper. In a bowl, toss the strawberries with the sugar, lemon juice, vanilla, and ⅛ teaspoon of salt. Spread the strawberries in an even layer on the prepared baking sheet. Roast, stirring once or twice, until the strawberries are tender and caramelized and the juices are syrupy, about 30 minutes. Transfer the strawberries and syrup to a bowl to cool. (The roasted fruit and syrup can be refrigerated in an airtight container for up to 1 week.)

To make the shortcakes, raise the oven temperature to 400°F (200°C). Line the baking sheet with a clean piece of parchment. In a bowl, whisk together the flour, baking powder, ½ teaspoon of salt, the sugar, and lemon zest until well blended. Using a pastry blender or 2 knives, cut in the butter until the pieces are about the size of peas. Add the cream and gently toss with a fork until the flour is just moistened and the ingredients are blended. Turn the dough out onto a lightly floured work surface. Gently press the dough into a thick rectangle about 6 by 4 inches (15 by 10 cm). Trim the edges even, then cut the dough into 6 equal squares.

Place the shortcakes on the prepared baking sheet, spacing them well apart. Brush each with a little cream, then sprinkle with sugar. Bake until puffed and golden, 15–18 minutes. Transfer the sheet to a wire rack and let cool for 5 minutes.

Split the shortcakes in half horizontally and place the bottom halves, cut side up, on plates. Spoon the strawberries and syrup over each half, dividing evenly among the halves, and top each with a dollop of whipped cream. Top with the remaining shortcake halves, cut side down, and serve.

# Mango Chile Ice Pops

Paletas (ice pops) come in nearly every flavor under the sun, ranging from sweet to spicy and savory to herbaceous. These chile-laced mango pops are a popular flavor in many paleterias, and papaya, passion fruit, or even blackberries and their juices all make exceptional substitutes for the mango. Use this same method without the chile powder for other flavors as well.

1 cup (8 fl oz/240 ml) mango juice or nectar

¼ cup (1¾ oz/50 g) sugar

2 teaspoons fresh lemon juice

1 teaspoon ancho chile powder

1 large mango, peeled, pitted, and diced

**MAKES 8 ICE POPS**

In a 1-qt (1-l) saucepan over medium-high heat, heat the mango juice, sugar, lemon juice, and ½ cup (4 fl oz/120 ml) water, stirring until the sugar dissolves. Transfer the mixture to a bowl and refrigerate until chilled, at least 2 hours.

Stir the ancho powder and diced mango into the chilled mixture and pour into eight 3-fl oz (90-ml) ice-pop molds. Insert an ice-pop stick into the center of each mold and freeze until the pops are solid, about 3 hours.

To release ice pops from their molds, run the bottoms of the molds briefly under cold water.

# Passion Fruit Cupcakes with Coconut Frosting

Intensely sour and sweet, fresh passion fruit has floral-citrus notes that are incredible in all types of desserts. Here, tender vanilla cupcakes are filled with a rich passion fruit curd, then topped with toasted-coconut frosting for a truly delightful treat.

**PASSION FRUIT CURD**

4 ripe passion fruits, or ¼ cup thawed frozen passion fruit pulp (seedless)

2 large egg yolks

⅓ cup (2½ oz/70 g) granulated sugar

Kosher salt

3 tablespoons unsalted butter, cut into pieces

**CUPCAKES**

1¾ cups (7½ oz/210 g) all-purpose flour

2 teaspoons baking powder

Kosher salt

¾ cup (6 oz/170 g) unsalted butter, at cool room temperature

⅔ cup (4¾ oz/140 g) granulated sugar

2 large eggs

1 cup (8 fl oz/240 ml) heavy cream

1 teaspoon vanilla extract

**MAKES 12 CUPCAKES**

To make the passion fruit curd, cut the passion fruits in half and scoop the pulp into a fine-mesh sieve set over a bowl. Press on the pulp to push it through the sieve; discard the seeds. Measure ¼ cup of pulp and juice and place in a small saucepan. Whisk in the egg yolks, sugar, and a pinch of salt. Cook over low heat, whisking constantly, until the mixture thickens and turns a bright orange-yellow (do not let it boil), 2–3 minutes. Remove from the heat, whisk in the butter, and then strain through a fine-mesh sieve into a bowl. Let cool for 15 minutes. Press a piece of plastic wrap directly onto the surface of the curd. Refrigerate until cold, about 2 hours.

To make the cupcakes, preheat the oven to 375°F (190°C). Line 12 standard muffin cups with paper liners. In a bowl, sift the flour, baking powder, and ½ teaspoon of salt together. In another bowl, using an electric mixer on low speed, beat the butter and sugar until blended, about 1 minute, then raise the speed to medium-high and beat until light and fluffy, 1–2 minutes. Beat in the eggs, one at a time. Reduce the speed to low and add the flour mixture in 3 additions, alternating with the cream in 2 additions, beginning and ending with the flour and beating just until blended after each addition. Beat in the vanilla. Divide the batter evenly among the prepared muffin cups, filling them nearly full. Bake until a toothpick inserted into the center of a cupcake comes out clean, about 20 minutes. Let the cupcakes cool in the pan for 10 minutes, then transfer to a wire rack and let cool completely.

## COCONUT FROSTING

½ cup (2 oz/60 g) shredded dried sweetened coconut

½ cup (4 oz/115 g) unsalted butter, at cool room temperature

3¾ cups (15 oz/425 g) confectioners' sugar

¼ cup (80 ml) coconut milk

To make the coconut frosting, reduce the oven temperature to 325°F (165°C). Spread the coconut in a single layer on a baking sheet and toast, stirring occasionally, until fragrant and lightly golden, about 5 minutes. Let cool completely.

In a bowl, using an electric mixer on medium-low speed, beat the butter with half of the confectioners' sugar until crumbly. Add the remaining confectioners' sugar and beat about 1 minute. With the mixer on medium speed, slowly add the coconut milk and beat until blended. Raise the speed to medium-high and beat the frosting until light and fluffy, about 1 minute.

Using a paring knife, cut a cone-shaped core about 1½ (4 cm) inches wide halfway down into the center of each cupcake. Gently remove the cores and set aside. Fill each cupcake with about 1 tablespoon of the curd. Trim the bottom off the cores and replace the tops of the cores. Spread the frosting over the top of the cupcakes and sprinkle with the toasted coconut. Let the frosting set for about 15 minutes before serving.

# Blackberry Slab Pie

A slab pie, baked in a rimmed baking sheet, is not only easier to make than a regular pie, it's also far less fussy to serve, and you can easily feed a crowd with it. Blackberry pie, especially when it's made with fresh-picked berries if you are lucky enough to live near a place to pick them, goes hand-in-hand with summer. But you can use any type of berry—raspberry, marionberry, olallieberry, blueberry—or even a mixture to create the slab pie of your dreams.

All-purpose flour, for dusting

Triple recipe Flaky Pie Dough (page 177), divided into 2 disks

1 cup (7 oz/200 g) sugar

¼ cup (1 oz/30 g) tapioca flour

2 teaspoons finely grated lemon zest

½ teaspoon ground cinnamon

Kosher salt

2 lb (1 kg) fresh blackberries, halved if large

3 tablespoons unsalted butter, cut into small pieces

**MAKES ABOUT 10 SERVINGS**

Place a rack in the lower third of the oven and preheat to 375°F (190°C).

On a lightly floured surface, roll out 1 dough disk into an 18-by-14-inch (45-by-35-cm) rectangle. Transfer to a rimmed baking sheet and gently press the dough into the bottom and up the sides of the pan. Roll out the other dough disk on a piece of parchment paper into a rectangle the same size as the first.

In a large bowl, gently stir together the sugar, tapioca, lemon zest, cinnamon, and ¼ teaspoon of salt. Add the blackberries and toss until evenly combined. Pour the filling into the crust in the pan and spread evenly. Dot with the butter. Using the parchment to help you, invert the rolled-out crust over the filling, lining up the edges. Peel off the parchment. Trim the dough edges, leaving a ¾-inch (2-cm) overhang. Fold the overhang under itself and crimp decoratively with your fingers or the tines of a fork. Cut a few steam vents in the top crust.

Bake until the crust is golden brown and the filling is bubbling, 45–50 minutes, tenting the pie edges with aluminum foil if the crust browns too quickly.

Let cool completely on a wire rack before serving, at least 2 hours. (The unbaked prepared pie can be covered tightly with aluminum foil and frozen for up to 2 weeks. Bake the frozen pie for an additional 10–15 minutes.)

# Cast-Iron Bittersweet Chocolate Cake

This rich, chocolatey cake is a snap to make, perfect for a weeknight "just because." The batter is stirred directly in the pan on the stovetop, then moved to the oven to bake. A buttery cocoa glaze makes an elegant finishing touch, but you can also leave it off and serve the cake dusted with powdered sugar. For a more complete dessert, serve with scoops of vanilla ice cream, fresh raspberries, and a sprinkling of flake salt.

## CHOCOLATE CAKE

¾ cup (5 oz/140 g) granulated sugar

½ cup (1½ oz/40 g) natural cocoa powder, sifted

Fine sea salt

4 large eggs

2 teaspoons vanilla extract

1 cup (4 oz/115 g) all-purpose flour

1 teaspoon baking soda

¾ cup (6 oz/170 g) unsalted butter, cut into pieces

4 oz (115 g) bittersweet chocolate, chopped

⅔ cup (5½ fl oz/160 ml) whole milk

## CHOCOLATE GLAZE

¼ cup (2 oz/60 g) unsalted butter

¼ cup (¾ oz/20 g) natural cocoa powder, sifted

2 tablespoons whole milk, plus more if needed

Fine sea salt

1 cup (4 oz/115 g) confectioners' sugar, sifted

½ teaspoon vanilla extract

**MAKES 8 SERVINGS**

Preheat the oven to 350°F (180°C).

To make the cake, in a bowl whisk together the granulated sugar, cocoa, and ½ teaspoon of salt. In another bowl, whisk together the eggs and vanilla. In a third bowl, whisk together the flour and baking soda.

In a 10-inch cast-iron skillet with at least 2-inch (5-cm) sides, melt the butter over low heat. Stir in the bittersweet chocolate just until it melts, then whisk in the milk. Remove from the heat. Add the cocoa mixture and whisk gently to combine, then add the egg mixture, whisking gently to combine. Carefully whisk in the flour mixture just until incorporated.

Transfer the cake to the oven and bake until a toothpick inserted into the center of the cake comes out clean, 27–30 minutes. Transfer the pan to a wire rack and let the cake cool to room temperature.

To make the glaze, in a small saucepan over low heat, melt the butter. Whisk in the cocoa powder, milk, and ⅛ teaspoon of salt. Remove from the heat. Add the confectioners' sugar and vanilla and whisk until smooth. The glaze should be thick but pourable; if it is too thick, add a little more milk, ¼ teaspoon at a time, to reach the desired consistency.

Pour the warm glaze over the top of the cake and spread evenly. Let stand until the glaze is set, about 1 hour. Serve wedges directly from the skillet.

# Ricotta Cheesecake with Blood Orange Marmalade

Ricotta cheesecake is lighter and more textured than the classic cheesecake. Here, the fluffy, creamy, orange-scented filling is topped with garnet-hued blood orange marmalade, creating a striking and delicious topping. The almond–graham cracker crust is a nice partner to the rich flavor of the cheesecake, but you can also use a standard graham cracker crust if you want to omit the nuts.

**CRUST**

1 cup (3½ oz/100 g) graham cracker crumbs

½ cup (2 oz/60 g) slivered almonds

3 tablespoons sugar

5 tablespoons (2½ oz/70 g) unsalted butter, melted

½ teaspoon vanilla extract

1 package (8 oz/225 g) cream cheese, cut into 4 pieces, at room temperature

7 oz (200 g) whole-milk ricotta, drained well

¾ cup (6 fl oz/180 ml) heavy cream

4 large eggs, separated

1 cup (7 oz/200 g) sugar

Finely grated zest of 1 orange

1 teaspoon vanilla extract

Kosher salt

½ cup (5 oz/140 g) blood orange or regular orange marmalade

**MAKES 8 TO 10 SERVINGS**

Preheat the oven to 350°F (180°C).

To make the crust, in a food processor, process the graham cracker crumbs, almonds, and sugar until finely ground. Add the melted butter and vanilla and process until the dry ingredients are evenly moistened. Transfer the crumb mixture to a 9-inch (23-cm) springform pan and press into the bottom and about 1½ (4 cm) inches up the sides. Bake until lightly browned, about 10 minutes. Let cool on a wire rack. Reduce the oven temperature to 300°F (150°C).

In the food processor, combine the cream cheese, ricotta, cream, egg yolks, sugar, orange zest, vanilla, and ⅛ teaspoon of salt. Process until smooth, 1–2 minutes. Pour into a large bowl. In another bowl, using an electric mixer on high speed, beat the egg whites until stiff peaks form. Using a rubber spatula, fold about a third of the egg whites into the cheese mixture and stir to incorporate. Then, gently fold in the remaining egg whites just until incorporated.

Pour the cheese mixture into the crust, smoothing the top. Bake for 30 minutes. Raise the oven temperature to 325°F (165°C) and continue baking until the surface is golden, the edges are firm, but the center still jiggles, 30–35 minutes. Turn off the oven, open the oven door, and let the cheesecake cool in the oven for about 3 hours. The center will fall slightly. Cover tightly with plastic wrap, being careful not to let the wrap touch the surface. Refrigerate for at least 12 hours or up to overnight.

To make the topping, in a small saucepan over low heat, warm the marmalade and 2–3 tablespoons of water to melt the marmalade. Set aside until cool.

Spread the topping evenly on top of the cheesecake. Remove the pan sides, transfer the cheesecake to a plate, and serve.

# Grilled Spiced Pineapple Kebabs with Rum Syrup

Fresh, ripe pineapple skewers are a fun treat at the end of a meal. These are served with a darkly sweet, rum-kissed syrup, but you can drizzle the pineapple with honey for a nonalcoholic version. Instead of skewers, cut the pineapple into thick slices crosswise, cut out the core, and grill the rings. Either way, the grilled pineapple is great with whipped cream.

2 tablespoons molasses

2 tablespoons honey

2 tablespoons dark rum

1 fresh pineapple

12 bamboo skewers, soaked in water for about 30 minutes

Avocado or canola oil, for brushing

3 tablespoons sugar

**MAKES 6 TO 8 SERVINGS**

In a small saucepan, whisk together the molasses, honey, and rum. Bring to a boil over medium heat and simmer until reduced slightly, 3–4 minutes.

Using a serrated knife, cut the pineapple in half lengthwise. Cut each half lengthwise into 6 wedges. Cut away and discard the core from each wedge. Place the wedges, skin side down, on a cutting board. Working with one wedge at a time, carefully run the knife between the skin and the flesh to separate the flesh. Cut the flesh crosswise into 6 equal chunks. Thread each chunk onto a skewer.

Prepare a gas or charcoal grill for direct grilling over high heat (450°–550°F/230°–290°C). Brush the grill grate clean.

Brush the fruit on all sides with avocado oil and sprinkle with the sugar. Grill the skewers directly over high heat, turning once, until grill marks appear, about 4 minutes per side. Transfer the skewers to a serving platter. Drizzle with the rum syrup and serve.

# Grilled Peaches with Salted Caramel Sauce

Grilled fruit is a natural end to a grilling party and, once you have the general method down, can be used in all sorts of ways. This recipe pairs grilled peaches with a homemade creamy caramel sauce, which is so delicious you might want to put it on everything. Choose ripe, fragrant peaches that are still slightly firm when pressed, and ideally, use late-season freestone fruits so the halves separate easily from the stone when cut and twisted. Serve with whipped cream or a scoop of vanilla ice cream.

**SALTED CARAMEL SAUCE**

1¼ cups (9 oz/250 g) sugar

1 teaspoon light corn syrup

¼ cup (2 fl oz/60 ml) heavy cream

1 tablespoon bourbon or 1 teaspoon vanilla extract

4 large ripe peaches

Flaky sea salt (optional)

**MAKES 4 SERVINGS**

To make the sauce, in a heavy saucepan over medium heat, combine the sugar, corn syrup, and 3 tablespoons water and stir until the sugar dissolves. Bring the mixture to a boil, stirring occasionally to make sure the caramel cooks evenly, until the syrup turns dark amber, about 5 minutes. Immediately pour in the cream (step back—there will be a lot of sputtering). When the bubbling subsides, stir the mixture until smooth. Stir in the bourbon, transfer to a heatproof container, and let cool.

Prepare a gas or charcoal grill for direct grilling over medium-high heat (400°–450°F/200°–230°C). Brush the grill grate clean.

Halve the peaches from the stem end to the blossom end and twist the halves in opposite directions to separate. Remove and discard the pits. Brush the peach halves all over with some of the caramel. Put the halves, cut side down, on the grate and cook, turning once, until nicely grill-marked on both sides, 2–3 minutes per side.

Transfer the peach halves, cut side up, to individual plates, placing 2 halves on each plate. Drizzle with the remaining caramel and top with a generous sprinkle of flaky salt, if using.

# Lemon Chiffon Gingersnap Pie

Fluffy and light, lemon chiffon pie is a timeless dessert made from a filling of lemon curd and whipped cream, stabilized with a little gelatin. This updated version swaps out the traditional graham cracker crust for a spicy gingersnap-cookie crust. Make the crumbs in a food processor or put the cookies into a resealable plastic bag and use a rolling pin to crush them.

1¼ cups (4 oz/115 g) gingersnap cookie crumbs

5 tablespoons (2½ oz/70 g) unsalted butter, melted

¾ cup (5 oz/140 g) plus 3 tablespoons granulated sugar

1 envelope (2¼ teaspoons) unflavored powdered gelatin

¾ cup (6 fl oz/180 ml) fresh lemon juice, strained

1 tablespoon finely grated lemon zest

4 large egg yolks, lightly beaten

Kosher salt

1¼ cups (10 fl oz/300 ml) heavy cream

¼ cup (1 oz/30 g) confectioners' sugar

**MAKES 8 SERVINGS**

Preheat the oven to 350°F (180°C). In a bowl, stir together the cookie crumbs, butter, and 3 tablespoons of granulated sugar until the crumbs are evenly moistened. Pat the crumb mixture firmly and evenly into the bottom and all the way up the sides of a 9-inch (23-cm) pie pan or dish. Bake until the crust is firm, 5–7 minutes.

Pour ¼ cup (2 fl oz/60 ml) cold water into a saucepan and sprinkle with the gelatin. Let stand until the gelatin softens and swells, 5–10 minutes. Whisk in the ¾ cup (5 oz/140 g) of granulated sugar, the lemon juice and zest, egg yolks, and ⅛ teaspoon of salt; the mixture will be lumpy. Cook over medium heat, stirring continuously, until the gelatin melts and the mixture thickens, 6–8 minutes. Do not allow the mixture to boil. Meanwhile, prepare a large bowl of ice water. Set the saucepan in an ice bath, stirring every so often, until the mixture is cool to the touch.

In a large bowl, using an electric mixer on medium-high speed, whip the cream and confectioners' sugar until thick, soft peaks form. Spoon the whipped cream into the gelatin mixture and fold together with a rubber spatula until smooth. Pour into the prepared crust, smoothing the top.

Refrigerate the pie until chilled and firm, at least 4 hours or up to overnight. Let stand at room temperature for 20 minutes before serving.

# Sour Cherry Cobblers

Fresh sour cherries have a short season, so if you find them at the market, scoop up as many as you can. If you can't find the tart fruits, look for frozen or jarred varieties packed in water (not syrup, and be sure to drain jarred cherries). These cobblers, each topped with a biscuit, are perfect with cold heavy cream poured over the top.

**CHERRY FILLING**

3 lb (1.4 kg) fresh sour cherries, pitted

⅓ cup (2½ oz/70 g) sugar

1 tablespoon fresh lemon juice

**BISCUIT TOPPING**

1½ cups (6½ oz/185 g) all-purpose flour

⅓ cup (2½ oz/70 g) plus 1 tablespoon sugar

1 teaspoon baking powder

½ teaspoon baking soda

Kosher salt

¾ teaspoon ground cinnamon

6 tablespoons (3 oz/90 g) cold unsalted butter, cut into ½-inch (12-mm) pieces

⅔ cup (5½ fl oz/160 ml) buttermilk

1 teaspoon vanilla extract

**MAKES 6 COBBLERS**

Preheat the oven to 375°F (190°C). Place six 1-cup (250-ml) ramekins or custard cups on a rimmed baking sheet.

To make the filling, in a large bowl, stir together the cherries, sugar, and lemon juice until well mixed. Divide the fruit mixture among the ramekins. Bake for 10 minutes.

To make the topping, in a large bowl, whisk together the flour, ⅓ cup (2½ oz/70 g) of sugar, the baking powder, baking soda, ½ teaspoon of salt, and ½ teaspoon of cinnamon. Using a pastry blender or 2 knives, cut in the butter until the mixture forms large, coarse crumbs the size of small peas. Pour the buttermilk and vanilla over the flour mixture and, using a wooden spoon, stir just until combined and a soft, sticky, evenly moistened dough forms.

Drop the dough by heaping spoonfuls onto the hot fruit, spacing it evenly over the surface. The topping will not cover the fruit but will spread during baking. In a small bowl, stir together the remaining 1 tablespoon of sugar and ¼ teaspoon of cinnamon. Sprinkle over the dough.

Bake until the fruit filling is bubbling, the topping is browned, and a toothpick inserted into the topping comes out clean, 30–35 minutes. Transfer the ramekins to a wire rack and let cool for 15 minutes. Serve warm.

# Rhubarb Ginger Crisp

Tart rhubarb and spicy ginger are close companions and a natural pair in this bubbling classic crisp with a crunchy oat topping. This crisp is a snap to make, and a warm bowlful topped with a scoop of vanilla ice cream is just the thing on a rainy spring evening. For a rhubarb-strawberry crisp, omit the ginger, and use 1 pound (450 g) rhubarb and 1 pound (450 g) hulled and sliced strawberries.

1½ lb (680 g) rhubarb stalks, cut into ¼-inch (6-mm) slices

1 cup (7 oz/200 g) granulated sugar

⅔ cup (3 fl oz/90 ml) fresh orange juice

Finely grated zest from 1 orange

1½ cups (6½ oz/185 g) all-purpose flour

¾ cup (5½ oz/155 g) firmly packed light brown sugar

½ cup (1¾ oz/50 g) quick-cooking rolled oats

3-inch (7.5-cm) piece fresh ginger, peeled and grated

½ teaspoon ground cinnamon

Kosher salt

6 tablespoons (3 oz/90 g) unsalted butter, melted and cooled

Vanilla ice cream, for serving

**MAKES 8 SERVINGS**

Preheat the oven to 375°F (190°C). In a 9-by-13-inch (23-by-33-cm) baking dish combine the rhubarb, sugar, orange juice, and zest. Toss the rhubarb mixture well, then spread it out evenly in the dish.

In a bowl, using a fork, stir together the flour, brown sugar, oats, ginger, cinnamon, and ¼ teaspoon of salt. Add the melted butter and stir until the ingredients are evenly moistened. Sprinkle the oat mixture evenly over the rhubarb.

Bake until the topping is golden brown and the juices are bubbling around the edges, about 30 minutes. Top with aluminum foil if the topping starts to get too brown. Transfer the dish to a wire rack and let cool, uncovered, for at least 20 minutes.

Serve warm or at room temperature. Spoon the warm crisp into bowls, top each with a scoop of ice cream, and serve right away.

# Grilled Banana Splits

Lightly grill-marked bananas are served slightly softened and warm in this ice cream parlor favorite. For the best result, choose just-ripe bananas that are still slightly firm with no black spots on the skins. And have fun experimenting with different flavors of ice cream and toppings, such as vanilla with caramel and chocolate sauce, or salted caramel ice cream with crumbled chocolate wafers.

4 ripe but firm bananas, peeled and halved lengthwise

2 tablespoons unsalted butter, melted

Chocolate and/or vanilla ice cream, or your favorite flavor, for serving

½ cup (4¼ oz/130 g) bittersweet chocolate sauce

Whipped Cream (page 177)

¼ cup (1 oz/30 g) chopped pecans or almonds, lightly toasted (optional)

**MAKES 4 SERVINGS**

Prepare a gas or charcoal grill for direct grilling over medium heat (350°–450°F/ 180°–230°C). Brush the grill grate clean.

Place the banana halves on a baking sheet and brush both sides with the melted butter. Place the banana halves, cut side down, directly over the heat. Grill until warm and grill-marked but not too soft, about 2 minutes. Transfer to the baking sheet.

To assemble, cut each banana half in half crosswise, then divide the bananas evenly among 4 shallow individual bowls. Top each with 1 or 2 scoops of ice cream, then drizzle with the chocolate sauce, dividing it evenly. Add a dollop of whipped cream and sprinkle with the pecans, if using. Serve at once.

# Tres Leches Cake

Tres leches is a wobbly, rich, meringue-topped cake that is enticingly decadent. A simple vanilla cake is doused with tres leches sauce, made from sweet condensed milk, evaporated milk, and cream. This version adds a hit of rum, but you can leave that out if you like. For an extra-special presentation, serve pieces garnished with sliced mango, papaya, or pineapple.

**CAKE**

½ cup (4 oz/115 g) vegetable shortening

1½ cups (10½ oz/300 g) sugar

2 large eggs

2¼ cups (10 oz/280 g) sifted all-purpose flour

2 teaspoons baking powder

Kosher salt

1 cup (8 fl oz/240 ml) whole milk

1 teaspoon vanilla extract

**TRES LECHES SAUCE**

1 can (14 fl oz/425 ml) sweetened condensed milk

1 can (12 fl oz/350 ml) evaporated milk

½ cup (4 fl oz/120 ml) heavy cream

3 tablespoons dark rum

1 teaspoon vanilla extract

**MERINGUE FROSTING**

¾ cup (5 oz/140 g) sugar

3 large egg whites

¼ teaspoon cream of tartar

**MAKES 10 TO 12 SERVINGS**

Preheat the oven to 350°F (180°C). Butter a 9-by-13-inch (23-by-33-cm) baking pan. Dust with flour, then tap out the excess.

To make the cake, in a bowl, using an electric mixer on high speed, beat the shortening until fluffy. Add the sugar a little at a time, beating until fluffy between additions. Reduce the speed to low and add the eggs one at a time, beating until well combined. Sift the flour, baking powder, and ½ teaspoon of salt into a large bowl. In a small bowl, whisk together the milk and vanilla. Add one-third of the milk mixture to the egg mixture and beat until well mixed, then add one-third of the flour mixture. Repeat twice more, beating well after each addition. Scrape the batter into the prepared pan.

Bake until a toothpick inserted into the center of the cake comes out clean, about 35 minutes. Let cool in the pan on a wire rack for 10 minutes, then invert the cake onto a platter and let cool completely.

To make the tres leches sauce, in a bowl, whisk together the condensed milk, evaporated milk, cream, rum, and vanilla. Poke the cake all over with a fork, and spoon the sauce over the surface, a little at a time, allowing the cake to absorb the sauce before adding more. A little sauce may pool on the platter, but the cake should absorb almost all of it. Cover the cake with plastic wrap and refrigerate for about 1 hour.

To make the frosting, in a saucepan over medium-high heat, bring the sugar and ½ cup (4 fl oz/120 ml) water to a boil, stirring to dissolve the sugar. Reduce the heat and simmer, brushing down the sides of the pan as crystals form with a pastry brush dipped in cold water. While the sugar is cooking, in a clean metal bowl, using an electric mixer on high speed, beat the egg whites and cream of tartar until stiff peaks form. Cook the sugar syrup until a candy thermometer registers 230°F (112°C), 10–12 minutes. Slowly add the boiling syrup in a thin stream to the beaten egg whites until all the syrup is incorporated. Continue beating until the meringue frosting is cooled and glossy. Spread the meringue frosting on the cake, cover, and refrigerate until well chilled, at least 3 hours and up to 8 hours. Serve chilled, cut into squares.

# S'mores Brownies

Chewy fudgy brownies just got better with the addition of honeyed graham crackers and melted, caramelized marshmallows. If s'mores aren't your thing, or you just have a craving for the classic, leave out the graham crackers and marshmallows. To cut the gooey brownies, let them cool completely, then fill a tall glass with hot water. Dip a knife in the water, wipe with a paper towel, then cut the brownies, dipping and wiping as you go. This also works well for sticky cakes or cookie bars.

1 cup (8 oz/225 g) unsalted butter, plus more for greasing

10 oz (285 g) bittersweet chocolate, minced

1 cup (7 oz/200 g) granulated sugar

¾ cup (5½ oz/155 g) firmly packed light brown sugar

4 large eggs

2 teaspoons vanilla extract

Kosher salt

1⅓ cups (5½ oz/155 g) cake flour

3 tablespoons natural cocoa powder

About 6 graham crackers, roughly crushed with your hands

About 12 jumbo marshmallows

**MAKES 12 BROWNIES**

Preheat the oven to 350°F (180°C). Generously butter a 9-by-13-inch (23-by-33-cm) baking dish.

In a saucepan over low heat, melt the butter and chocolate, stirring often. Remove from the heat and whisk in the granulated sugar and brown sugar. Whisk in the eggs one at a time, beating well after each addition. Whisk in the vanilla and 1 teaspoon of salt.

Sift the flour and cocoa over the chocolate mixture and, using a rubber spatula, stir in until just blended. Stir in the graham crackers. Pour into the prepared dish and spread evenly.

Bake for 20 minutes, then remove the pan from the oven and top with the marshmallows. Continue to bake until a toothpick inserted into the center comes out almost completely clean, 10–15 minutes longer. Transfer the dish to a wire rack and let cool, then cut into gooey squares.

drinks

# Michelada

Perfect for a warm day on the beach, these beer cocktails are kind of like beer Bloody Marys. A spicy mixture of Clamato juice or tomato juice, hot-pepper sauce, lime, and Worcestershire sauce combine to form this refreshing and flavorful drink.

Coarse sea salt

2 teaspoons chile powder

5 limes

8 fl oz (240 ml) Clamato juice or tomato juice

2 tablespoons hot-pepper sauce

4 teaspoons Worcestershire sauce

4 bottles (12 fl oz/350 ml each) Mexican beer, such as Dos Equis or Pacifico

**MAKES 4 MICHELADAS**

Spread the 2 tablespoons of salt and the chile powder on a small, flat plate. Cut 1 lime into 5 wedges. Moisten the rims of 4 tall glasses or tumblers with 1 lime wedge and dip each rim into the chile salt to coat it evenly. Save the remaining 4 lime wedges for garnish.

Juice the remaining 4 limes; you should have about ½ cup of lime juice. In a pitcher, gently stir together the lime juice, Clamato juice, hot-pepper sauce, and Worcestershire sauce. Fill the glasses with ice cubes. Pour the Clamato juice mixture into the glasses, top each with the beer, garnish each with a lime wedge, and serve.

# Lime Margaritas

This recipe for an on-the-rocks version only has a few ingredients, so be sure to use a good-quality tequila that tastes nice and smooth. Instead of the triple sec, you can also sweeten the margaritas to taste with agave, the same plant used to make tequila.

Kosher salt

1 large lime

1 cup (8 fl oz/240 ml) tequila blanco

½–¾ cup (4–6 fl oz/ 120–180 ml) triple sec, or more as desired

½ cup (4 fl oz/120 ml) fresh lime juice

**MAKES 4 MARGARITAS**

Spread 2 tablespoons of salt on a small, flat plate. Cut the lime into 5 wedges. Moisten the rims of 4 rocks glasses with 1 lime wedge and dip each rim into the salt to coat it evenly. Fill the glasses with ice.

In a pitcher stir together the tequila, triple sec, and lime juice. Pour the margaritas into the glasses, dividing it evenly. Garnish each glass with the remaining lime wedges and serve.

# Minty Mojitos

There's nothing quite so summery as the smell of fresh mint on a hot day. It's the base of these herbaceous cocktails, where fresh mint leaves are muddled with lime and simple syrup to release the intoxicating aroma. Use a light or golden rum for these Cuban cocktails.

Leaves from 1 bunch fresh mint, plus 4 sprigs for garnish

1 tablespoon Simple Syrup (page 177)

½ cup (4 fl oz/120 ml) fresh lime juice

1 cup (8 fl oz/240 ml) golden rum

4 lime wheels, for garnish

**MAKES 4 MOJITOS**

In a pitcher, combine the mint leaves, simple syrup, and lime juice and muddle until the mint is broken up. Add the rum and stir until well mixed. Fill 4 highball glasses with crushed ice. Pour the mojito into the glasses, dividing it evenly. Garnish each glass with a lime wheel and a mint sprig and serve.

# Strawberry Lillet Vodka Soda

This is a great use of strawberries that might be a little past their best since most of them are crushed into the cocktail with a muddler. Lillet is an orange-flavored fortified wine that pairs beautifully with the berries, a hint of lime, and some fizzy club soda. For a less intense cocktail, leave out the vodka, and increase the Lillet by ¼ cup (2 fl oz/60 ml) and the club soda by ½ cup (4 fl oz/120 ml).

12 strawberries, sliced

¼ cup (2 fl oz/60 ml) Simple Syrup (page 177)

¼ cup (2 fl oz/60 ml) fresh lime juice

¾ cup (6 fl oz/180 ml) vodka

½ cup (4 fl oz/120 ml) Lillet

1 cup (8 fl oz/240 ml) club soda

4 lime wedges

**MAKES 4 COCKTAILS**

Reserve 4 strawberry slices for garnish. In a cocktail shaker, muddle the remaining strawberries, simple syrup, and lime juice until the strawberries are crushed. Add the vodka, Lillet, and ice. Cover, shake vigorously, and strain into 4 ice-filled collins or highball glasses. Top each with club soda. Garnish each with a lime wedge and a reserved strawberry slice and serve.

# Rosé Sangria with Citrus & Raspberries

Sangria is a traditional Spanish staple made from red or white wine and garnished with citrus fruits and apples. This variation uses rosé, and is perfect for sipping on a lazy weekend. For a less potent sangria, add more juice.

1 bottle (750 ml) rosé wine

1 cup (8 fl oz/240 ml) fresh grapefruit juice

½ cup (4 fl oz/120 ml) fresh orange juice

⅓ cup (3 fl oz/90 ml) Cointreau

⅓ cup (3 fl oz/90 ml) brandy

¼ cup (2 fl oz/60 ml) Simple Syrup (page 177)

1 *each,* lemon and orange

4 cups (1 lb/450 g) raspberries

¾ cup (6 fl oz/180 ml) soda water

**MAKES 8 SANGRIAS**

In a large pitcher, combine the wine, grapefruit juice, orange juice, Cointreau, brandy, and simple syrup and stir until blended. Cut the lemon and orange into ½-inch (12-mm) slices, then stir in the lemon and orange slices and the raspberries. Refrigerate for at least 1 hour or up to 8 hours.

Pour the soda water into the sangria and stir to combine. Pour the sangria into ice-filled wine glasses and serve.

# Blackberry Lemonade Whiskey Sour

Whiskey sours are an old-fashioned cocktail made from whiskey, lemon juice, and sugar. This dressed-up version includes a frothy egg white layer and a sweet blackberry-lemon coulis. Be sure to choose a sweet sherried whiskey, not a smoky one.

4 cups (1 lb/450 g) fresh blackberries

¾ cup (6 fl oz/180 ml) plus 2 tablespoons fresh lemon juice

1 cup (8 fl oz/240 ml) whiskey

½ cup (4 fl oz/120 ml) Simple Syrup (page 177)

1 large egg white

4 lemon twists

**MAKES 4 COCKTAILS**

In a blender, combine the blackberries and 2 tablespoons of lemon juice and blend until smooth. Strain the blackberry coulis through a fine-mesh sieve into a container; you should have ½ cup. Use at once or cover and refrigerate for up to 2 days.

In a cocktail shaker, combine the whiskey, ¾ cup (6 fl oz/180 ml) of lemon juice, the simple syrup, blackberry coulis, and egg white. Cover and shake vigorously, then open the shaker and add ice. Cover and shake vigorously again. Place 1 large ice cube into each of 4 chilled rocks glasses. Strain the cocktail into the glasses. Garnish each with a lemon twist.

# Watermelon Agua Frescas

When you want an extra-refreshing nonalcoholic drink, these agua frescas are just the thing. Purée fresh watermelon, a little lime, and just enough simple syrup to sweeten and you will be the star of the party. Top with sparkling water for a little extra pizzazz.

3 lb (1.4 kg) peeled, seeded, and cubed watermelon (about 8 cups)

¼ cup (2 fl oz/60 ml) fresh lime juice

¼ cup (2 fl oz/60 ml) Simple Syrup (page 177)

About 2 cups (16 fl oz/475 ml) still or sparkling water

Sugar (optional)

**MAKES 8 AGUA FRESCAS**

Place 4 cups (1½ lb/680 g) of watermelon in a blender and blend until smooth. Add lime juice to taste and half of the simple syrup and blend until well mixed. Refrigerate until well chilled. Pour the purée into a large pitcher. Add the remaining 4 cups (1½ lb/680 g) of watermelon, more lime juice to taste, and the remaining simple syrup to the blender and blend until smooth, then add to the pitcher. Stir well and add water to thin the mixture to the desired consistency. Taste and adjust the flavor with sugar or more lime juice if needed. Serve in tall glasses over ice.

# Meyer Lemon–Rosemary Moscow Mule

The Moscow mule is traditionally a simple cocktail of vodka, lime, and ginger beer. This version uses sweet, fragrant Meyer lemon instead of lime, and adds a hit of rosemary for a light herbaceous note. A copper mug is traditional, but a rocks glass will do.

1 cup (8 fl oz/240 ml) vodka

½ cup (4 fl oz/120 ml) fresh Meyer lemon juice

¼ cup (2 fl oz/60 ml) Rosemary Simple Syrup (page 177)

12 fl oz (350 ml) ginger beer

4 fresh rosemary sprigs

4 lemon slices

**MAKES 4 COCKTAILS**

In a cocktail shaker filled with ice, combine the vodka, lemon juice, and rosemary simple syrup. Cover, shake vigorously, and strain into 4 ice-filled copper mugs. Top each cocktail with ginger beer. Garnish with a rosemary sprig and a lemon slice and serve.

# BASICS

## PIZZA DOUGH

**MAKES 1 LB (450 G) DOUGH, ENOUGH FOR FOUR 10-INCH (25-CM) PIZZAS**

1 cup (8 fl oz/240 ml) warm water (110°–115°F/43°C–46°C)

1 envelope (2¼ teaspoons) active dry yeast

1 teaspoon sugar

4 tablespoons (2 fl oz/60 ml) extra-virgin olive oil

Kosher salt

2¾ cups (11½ oz/325 g) bread flour, plus more for kneading and dusting

In a large bowl, stir together the water, yeast, and sugar. Let stand until foamy, about 5 minutes. Stir in 3 tablespoons of the olive oil, 1½ teaspoons of salt, and the flour until the dough comes together.

Turn the dough out onto a lightly floured work surface and knead until the dough is smooth and elastic, about 5 minutes. Add more flour as needed to keep the dough from sticking to your hands or the work surface, but try to add as little flour as possible. Shape the dough into a ball.

Coat a large bowl with the remaining 1 tablespoon of olive oil. Put the dough in the bowl and then turn the dough to coat it with oil. Cover the bowl with plastic wrap and let the dough rise in a warm spot (about 90°F/32°C) until doubled in bulk, about 1 hour. Or, for more complex flavor, place the bowl in the refrigerator and let the dough rise overnight, then bring the dough back to room temperature before rolling it out. To freeze the dough, cut it into 4 pieces and shape each piece into a somewhat flat disk. Place each disk in a resealable plastic bag and press out the air. Seal the bag and freeze for up to 1 month. To use, thaw in a bowl of cold water for a few hours or thaw in the refrigerator overnight. Bring the dough to room temperature before rolling it out.

## PIZZA SAUCE

**MAKES ABOUT 3 CUPS (24 FL OZ/700 ML)**

1 can (28 oz/800 g) crushed tomatoes

2 tablespoons balsamic vinegar

2 tablespoons extra-virgin olive oil

2 teaspoons Italian seasoning or dried oregano

In a bowl, stir together all of the ingredients. Use immediately or transfer to an airtight container and refrigerate for up to 1 week or freeze for up to 1 month.

## BASIL PESTO

**MAKES ABOUT 1 CUP (8 FL OZ/240 ML)**

1 clove garlic, chopped

¼ cup (1 oz/30 g) pine nuts

2 cups (2 oz/60 g) packed fresh basil leaves

½ cup (4 fl oz/120 ml) extra-virgin olive oil

½ cup (2 oz/60 g) freshly grated Parmesan cheese

Kosher salt and freshly ground pepper

With a food processor running, drop the garlic through the feed tube and process until minced. Turn off the processor, add the pine nuts, and pulse a few times to chop. Add the basil and pulse a few times to chop coarsely. Then, with the processor running, add the olive oil through the feed tube in a slow, steady steam and process until a smooth, moderately thick paste forms, stopping to scrape down the sides of the bowl as needed. Transfer to a bowl and stir in the Parmesan. Season to taste with salt and pepper.

# BASIC BARBECUE RUB

**MAKES ½ CUP (1¾ OZ/50 G)**

2 tablespoons smoked paprika

2 tablespoons light brown sugar

1 tablespoon kosher salt

2 teaspoons freshly ground pepper

2 teaspoons onion powder

2 teaspoons dry mustard

1 teaspoon cayenne pepper

In a small bowl, stir together all of the ingredients. Store in an airtight container at room temperature for up to 1 month.

# CLASSIC BARBECUE SAUCE

**MAKES ABOUT 3 CUPS (24 FL OZ/700 ML)**

2 cups (16 oz/450 g) ketchup, store-bought or homemade (page 176)

3 tablespoons dark brown sugar

3 tablespoons apple cider vinegar

2 tablespoons yellow mustard

2 tablespoons Worcestershire sauce

2 teaspoons smoked paprika

1½ teaspoons kosher salt

1 teaspoon garlic powder

½ teaspoon onion powder

½ teaspoon freshly ground pepper

In a saucepan over high heat, combine all of the ingredients and bring to a boil. Reduce the heat to medium-low and simmer until slightly thickened, about 20 minutes. Use immediately or let cool, transfer to an airtight container, and refrigerate for up to 1 month.

# WESTERN CAROLINA BARBECUE SAUCE

**MAKES ABOUT 3¼ CUPS (26 FL OZ/650 ML)**

2 cups (16 fl oz/475 ml) apple cider vinegar

¾ cup (6 oz/170 g) ketchup, store-bought or homemade (page 176)

½ cup (4 fl oz/120 ml) water

2 tablespoons sugar

1 tablespoon mild hot-pepper sauce, such as Frank's RedHot

2 teaspoons kosher salt

1 teaspoon red pepper flakes

½ teaspoon freshly ground pepper

In a saucepan over medium heat, combine all of the ingredients and bring to a simmer, stirring often. Remove from the heat and use immediately or let cool, transfer to an airtight container, and refrigerate for up to 1 month.

# PEACH BOURBON BARBECUE SAUCE

**MAKES ABOUT 3 CUPS (24 FL OZ/700 ML)**

2 cups (16 oz/450 g) ketchup, store-bought or homemade (page 176)

3 tablespoons dark brown sugar

3 tablespoons apple cider vinegar

2 tablespoons *each* yellow mustard and Worcestershire sauce

2 teaspoons smoked paprika

1½ teaspoons kosher salt

1 teaspoon garlic powder

½ teaspoon onion powder

½ teaspoon freshly ground pepper

1 cup (8 fl oz/240 ml) peach nectar

½ cup (4 fl oz/120 ml) bourbon

4 tablespoons (2 oz/60 g) unsalted butter

2 tablespoons dark (not blackstrap) molasses

In a saucepan over high heat, combine all of the ingredients and bring to a boil. Reduce the heat to medium-low and simmer until slightly thickened, about 20 minutes. Use immediately or let cool, transfer to an airtight container, and refrigerate for up to 1 month. If the sauce has been refrigerated, reheat over low heat before using.

## SMOKY TOMATO SALSA

**MAKES ABOUT 1½ CUPS (9 OZ/250 G)**

3 large, ripe tomatoes, thickly sliced

1 small red onion, thickly sliced

1 jalapeño chile, halved lengthwise and seeded

Extra-virgin olive oil, for drizzling

Juice of 2 limes

¼ cup (½ oz/15 g) minced fresh cilantro

Kosher salt and freshly ground pepper

Prepare a gas or charcoal grill for direct grilling over high heat (450°–550°F/230°–290°C). Brush the grill grate clean. Drizzle the tomato and onion slices and chile halves with olive oil. Place on the grill and cook, turning once, until some nice char develops, about 2 minutes per side. Remove from the grill, chop coarsely, and place in a bowl. Stir in the lime juice and cilantro. Divide the mixture in half. Place half of the mixture in a food processor and purée, then return to the bowl. Mix well and season with salt and pepper. The salsa tastes best if made a day in advance. It will keep, covered and refrigerated, for up to 1 week.

## ROASTED TOMATO DRESSING

**MAKES ABOUT 1 CUP (8 FL OZ/240 ML)**

1 lb (450 g) ripe plum tomatoes, cored and quartered lengthwise

2 cloves garlic, minced

5 tablespoons (2½ fl oz/75 ml) extra-virgin olive oil

Kosher salt

¼ cup (2 fl oz/60 ml) red wine vinegar

1 tablespoon sweet paprika

1 tablespoon mayonnaise

Preheat the oven to 400°F (200°C). On a rimmed baking sheet, combine the tomatoes and garlic, drizzle with 1 tablespoon of olive oil, and toss to coat evenly. Spread the tomatoes in a single layer on the pan and sprinkle with a little salt. Roast the tomatoes until softened and slightly shriveled, about 30 minutes.

Let the tomatoes cool completely and then transfer to a food processor. Add the vinegar, paprika, mayonnaise, and the remaining 4 tablespoons (2 fl oz/60ml) of olive oil and process until smooth. Use immediately or transfer to an airtight container and store in the refrigerator for up to 2 weeks.

## HOMEMADE KETCHUP

**MAKES ABOUT 1½ CUPS (12 FL OZ/350 ML)**

1 can (28 oz/875 g) crushed Roma tomatoes

¼ cup (1¼ oz/40 g) light corn syrup

3 tablespoons cider vinegar

2 tablespoons minced yellow corn

2 tablespoons minced red bell pepper

1 small clove garlic, minced

1 tablespoon firmly packed golden brown sugar

1 teaspoon kosher salt

⅛ teaspoon freshly ground pepper

Pinch each ground allspice, ground cloves, celery seeds, and yellow mustard seeds

½ bay leaf

In a saucepan over medium heat, combine all of the ingredients and bring to a boil, stirring. Reduce the heat to medium-low and simmer, stirring frequently, until the mixture thickens and has reduced by half, about 1 hour.

Rub the ingredients through a medium-mesh sieve into a heatproof bowl, discarding any solids. Let cool. Transfer to an airtight container and refrigerate overnight to allow the flavors to blend before using. Use right away or refrigerate for up to 2 weeks.

## CHIMICHURRI

**MAKES ABOUT 1 CUP (8 FL OZ/240 ML)**

1 cup (1 oz/30 g) packed fresh flat-leaf parsley leaves and small stems

1 cup (1 oz/30 g) packed fresh cilantro leaves and small stems

⅓ cup (90 ml) extra-virgin olive oil

¼ small red bell pepper, seeded and coarsely chopped

3 cloves garlic, coarsely chopped

2 tablespoons coarsely chopped yellow onion

½ teaspoon dried oregano

¼–½ teaspoon red pepper flakes

Kosher salt

3 tablespoons sherry vinegar

In a food processor, combine the parsley, cilantro, olive oil, ¼ cup (2 fl oz/60 ml) water, bell pepper, garlic, onion, oregano, red pepper flakes, and 1 teaspoon of salt and process until finely chopped but not completely puréed, stopping once to scrape down the sides of the bowl. Use immediately or transfer to an airtight container and store in the refrigerator for up to 2 days. Stir in the vinegar just before serving.

## SRIRACHA MAYO

**MAKES 1 CUP (8 FL OZ/240 ML)**

¾ cup (6 fl oz/180 ml) mayonnaise

¼ cup (2 fl oz/60 ml) Sriracha

Finely grated zest and juice of 1 lime

In a bowl, combine all of the ingredients and mix well. Use immediately or transfer to an airtight container and store in the refrigerator for up to 2 weeks.

## SIMPLE SYRUP

**MAKES ABOUT 1½ CUPS (12 FL OZ/350 ML)**

1 cup (8 fl oz/240 ml) water

1 cup (7 oz/200 g) sugar

In a small saucepan over medium-high heat, bring the water to a simmer. Add the sugar and stir until the sugar is dissolved. Remove from the heat and let cool. Strain the syrup through a fine-mesh sieve into a clean container, cover, and refrigerate for up to 2 weeks.

**ROSEMARY SIMPLE SYRUP:** *Add 5 fresh rosemary sprigs, coarsely chopped, to the water along with the sugar.*

## FLAKY PIE DOUGH

**MAKES ENOUGH FOR ONE 9-INCH (23-CM) SINGLE CRUST PIE**

1⅓ cups (5½ oz/155 g) all-purpose flour

Kosher salt

½ cup (4 oz/115 g) cold unsalted butter, cut into cubes

¼ cup (2 fl oz/60 ml) ice water, plus more as needed

In a food processor, combine the flour and ¼ teaspoon of salt. Pulse 2 or 3 times to mix the ingredients evenly. Add the butter and pulse 8 to 10 times, until the butter pieces are the size of peas. Add the ice water and pulse 10 to 12 times. Stop the machine and squeeze a piece of dough. If it crumbles, add more ice water, 1 tablespoon at a time, and pulse just until the dough holds together when pinched. When the dough is ready, it should come together in a rough mass in the food processor bowl but not form a ball. Do not overmix or the crust will be tough. Transfer the dough to a work surface and shape into a disk. Wrap well in plastic wrap and refrigerate for at least 1 hour or up to 1 day.

## WHIPPED CREAM

**MAKES ABOUT 1 CUP (8 FL OZ /240 ML)**

1 cup (8 fl oz/240 ml) heavy cream

2 tablespoons sugar

½ teaspoon vanilla extract

In a bowl, using an electric mixer on medium speed, whip the cream, sugar, and vanilla until medium peaks form, about 5 minutes. Use right away or cover with plastic wrap and refrigerate until ready to use, up to 4 hours. Whisk the cream briefly before using.

# INDEX